Riches from Wragg

Riches from Wragg

E.C. Wragg
Professor of Education
Exeter University

tɓ
Trentham Books

First published in 1990 by Trentham Books

Trentham Books Limited
13/14 Trent Trading Park
Botteslow Street
Stoke-on-Trent
Staffordshire
England ST1 3LY

British Library Cataloguing in Publication Data
Wragg E.C. (Ted)
  Riches from Wragg
  1. Education. Humour
  I. Title
  370

ISBN: 0 948080 43 4

Designed and typeset by Trentham Print Design Limited, Chester
and printed in Great Britain by BPCC Wheatons Ltd, Exeter.

iv

Contents

Chapter 5: LMS — Lots More Suffering

Chapter 6: A Governors' Guide to...

Chapter 7: Politics, politics

Chapter 1:

The Rise and Fall of Mr Bun

The proper use of the B-day

It was quite a shock to see my 13-year old son applying the contents of a tube of Brylcreem to his hair. The first thought to hit me was that I had missed some obscure clause in Mr Bun's Education Act which made slicking back the locks a compulsory component of the national curriculum for third- years. The whole country would eventually be teeming with millions of beaming clones of Old Smoothie. Just when I had begun to work out the in- service implications of such a move, I discovered the much more innocent explanation was that the gel version of our traditional hair-cream has become popular with trendy adolescents. It was as well that no further demands were to be made on in-service resources, because the implications of the 1988 Education Act will swallow most of the budget for years to come. Forget about doing anything of your choice on the professional development front. Learning Bunspeak will be the top priority.

Mr Bun has already announced that there will be a magic number which will apply to in-service programmes. The number two will dominate all. For a start the induction courses will last precisely two days. This is based on the contemptuous notion that any fool can teach, so a couple of days for senior people gives sufficient information.

They can then go back to their colleagues and sprinkle it on them in a couple of hours. This was the pattern which turned out to be so inadequate for the GCSE. It was called the cascade method of training, but some people named it the piston model. If the subtlety of that epithet is not apparent, try saying it with a pause before the last two letters.

I wonder if the magic number two is used by other professions for important new initiatives. Perhaps it is the way heart transplant surgery is taught. Day one: how to remove a person's heart. Day two: how to put someone else's back in so no one will notice. No doubt the engineers do it as well. Day one: how to build a suspension bridge. Day two: how to stick it back up again when it has fallen down.

For those eager to know Mr Bun's plans for these two riveting days, I can reveal that a secret copy of the National Double B-day Festival has fallen into my hands. In in-service patois, Baker Days are known as B-days on the grounds that although everyone knows what they are, no one knows how to use them properly (B-days — bidets, geddit?)

The magic number two dominates everything. The first day begins with 'an explanation of the intellectual reasoning behind the Education Act'.

This lasts two minutes, to allow the speaker to cover the topic twice.

Next we move on to the national curriculum. Teachers will learn how to teach the two national songs. "Greensleeves" (Primary) and "Land of Hope and Glory" (secondary), and how to do a literary criticism of the two national poems — both from Mr Bun's Bumper Funbook of English Verse, which will be a set book — "Wee Willie Winkie" (Primary) and the clean version of "The boy stood on the burning deck" (secondary)

In the lit crit session there will be an explanation of how "Wee Willie Winkie" is actually an ode to Government social policy. The "Willie" was in fact William Whitelaw when he was Home Secretary, touring the inner cities each evening disguised as an enormous marquee looking for candidates who needed a short, sharp shock. Compulsory going-to-bed at eight o'clock comes in the Government's family responsibility programme.

Day One ends with a two-hour session on national testing at 7,11,14 and 16. The first hour will show teachers how to draw ticks and crosses and put in detention those with low marks. The second hour is entitled "How-to-deal-with-angry-and-upset-parents-of-seven- year-olds-who-have-had-many-sleepless-nights-and-wonder-if-their- child-is-a-complete-moron-and-who-thought-up-this-bloody-stupid-notion-anyway".

Day two covers raising money when your school is bankrupt because it was inadequately resourced under local financial management. This consists of sessions on "how to organize a raffle", "the teacher as busker", "bank robbery for beginners" (including "which end to saw off your shotgun" for CDT teachers), and "seven painless methods of suicide". For schools opting out of local authority control there will be a lecture on what the Government will do to help, entitled "You're on your own now, matey".

Two higher degrees can be obtained. Those who attend day one will be awarded the degree of MB (Master of Bunspeak), and completing both days gains the MBA (Master of Bugger All). Where contempt for professional skill and pride is concerned, two days, two hours, two minutes, two degrees, two fingers, what's the difference?

Two words for Mr Baker

I have always enjoyed September. In Devon, where I live, it is the most beautiful month, and I cannot escape childhood memories of coming back from the holidays and looking for conkers at the start of the school year. Not that there were too many in central Sheffield when I was a child, but we wrestled over the few to be found in the local parks, baked them, soaked them in vinegar, even kept them in a drawer for months. Nowadays kids probably laser them.

Then there was the hilarious spectacle of going back to school and seeing all one's mates who had gone into the adolescent growth spurt during the summer holidays, wandering round, beetroot-faced, wearing hopelessly ill-fitting uniforms they had only taken out of the wardrobe the night before. I loved it all and the conkers remind me of it each autumn. It makes the start of school much more interesting than another year back at the ball-bearing factory, though the production line view of education would seek to change all that.

One of the many unpredicted (by the Government that is) consequences of the 1988 Education Act is the nature of the schools that want to opt out and acquire grant maintained status. My guess is that, of the first 100 to try to defect, some 80 will be small schools or grammar schools under threat of closure, another 15 will want to become Muslim schools, and only five will be the sort of snobby up-market compers that the Government hoped would lead the non-existent rush.

This places the Secretary of state in a dilemma. Does he allow non-viable schools to stay open, thus countermanding his own department's circulars about turning surplus schools into warehouses, massage parlours and Porsche repair shops, or does he turn them down, thereby arousing the wrath of parents?

I can imagine that when the position becomes clearer there will be a large pile of embarrassing decisions on his desk. One factor will no doubt be politics. A sitting MP or ruling council friendly to the Government will get a warmer response than if one of the opposition parties is in power locally.

If the DES is selling tickets for the public to witness this embarrassing moment, then bags I one on the front row. If it is to be private mourners only, then I will offer these two words of condolence. Tee hee.

*   *   *

I have just received one of the cleverest put-downs ever. It was very skilfully done in response to an article I had written. The topic was the proposal to introduce a voucher system into higher education.

I had argued that the voucher scheme would bring chaos, fashions would dictate policy, staff would be made redundant, buildings become empty or overcrowded, as subjects like accountancy would first boom and then collapse.

"I was very interested in your article," the letter began. I preened myself at the prospect of a minor piece of fan mail. "I have always been opposed to a voucher scheme myself" (Ah, a friend as well as a fan). "However," it went on, "I had not realised the arguments against it were so weak". Brilliant.

True confessions of a schoolie

I have a confession to make. Like a small but significant section of the population, I am a schoolaholic. We "schoolies", as the press have dubbed us, (well, they haven't actually, but it can only be a matter of time) have an irresistible need to find a school wherever we happen to be. Stick me in downtown Benidorm on a hot August afternoon and I will sniff out Benidorm County Primary School for you in minutes.

Schoolies can usually be found peering through windows, eager to discover if Class B is doing yet another project on dinosaurs, or is it volcanoes, or skulking round staffrooms checking whether the bridge four has yet deigned to go and teach 3C a full 10 minutes after the bell, or if that rotting jockstrap we noticed on top of the lockers on our last visit has been incinerated. There is no known cure, though Edwina Currie has asked HMI to knit woollen bags for us to wear over our heads.

Some sufferers cannot resist reading anything describing education in other countries. Up-market patients call this "Comparative Education", but we working-class schoolies just persuade ourselves there is a lot to learn from other lands.

A few weeks ago I was perusing *The TES,* hoping no one would notice I was the only person in the room not reading the "Situations Vacant" section, when my eyes lit upon an astonishing story from China. It is not a spoof. I have checked.

The account began: "Teachers in China are selling pickled eggs and working as dancing partners after class in order to supplement their low wages." Now although this will be terrific news for my old friends, the British Egg Information Service, who are frantically trying to get eggs into the national curriculum, I can only guess that Chinese teachers must be less lethal on the ballroom floor than their British counterparts.

In my experience many teachers, especially union reps at annual conferences, become complete psychopaths once loudspeakers are switched on and the rhythmic pulse of the music reaches the darkest depths of their id. Heads are worse. I was in traction for months after one NAHT do. Not so much *Come Dancing* as *Come Crippling*.

The story goes on to tell how low wages have led to a teacher supply crisis in China. The Government decreed that if schools needed more cash they would have to find it through entrepreneurial activities. A frisson of deep suspicion was already entering my mind, so I read on eagerly.

"Mr He Dongchang, the Minister of Education, claims that since 1978, state spending on education has gone up 15.3 per cent every year. In 1987 expenditure was 27 billion yuan...".

Now hold on a minute, little sunbeam. He Dongchang my foot. Before you drown me in more telephone numbers, come clean. Admit, Kenneth Baker, that you have been moonlighting over the other side of the globe as He Glib Bun, aided by She Rum Bold and She Thatch Her, as part of a state export drive for Bunthink.

What we schoolies do discover from meeting overseas teachers and occasional visits, is that life elsewhere is not always as rosy as we are given to believe. The popular mythology about West Germany, for example, is that it is awash with brilliant classroom skills.

There is indeed much to learn from the excellent vocational education at all levels and the high-quality work with children of average and below average ability. But the Gymnasium, the school for more able pupils, has suffered from some unspeakably brain-corroding and monotonous teaching.

The German university system, with its meandering open-ended degrees, huge classes and lack of tutorial contact for students, is a good model of what not to do. The probationer teacher is no fresh-faced 22 year old, but, after an eternal undergraduate course and national service, a wizened middle-aged character who looks like a candidate for early retirement.

Another interesting argument we schoolies like to pursue is whether enterprise can be taught directly or is acquired obliquely. I once spent 10 days on a schoolie safari watching classes in Hong Kong. The level of industry was formidable, but the challenge to the imagination zero. Mostly pupils copied out work or listened to the teacher.

When they left school to start a shirt-sewing business it was probably out of relief. Education had given them one essential ingredient of enterprise, the capacity for hard work, but not the crucial other, imagination. As a result, most businesses involved routine rather than invention.

British resourcefulness and originality have been nurtured because teachers were unafraid to develop these qualities in children. Though there is much to be gained by studying the best practice from elsewhere, we should

6

lose a great deal if the over slavish application of He Glib Bun's national curriculum merely produced a set of identikit national clones.

"Let us ask the Minister about his views on on abolishing 'A' Levels'

The farce of the flashlight brigade

There was a distinct sense of gloom among the conference of primary heads I was addressing. They had just heard on the radio that Mr Bun, fresh from his trans-Siberian tour of photo opportunities, had announced in his speech to the Conservative Party conference that he was going to restore traditional teaching to primary schools, whatever that might have meant.

Most seemed afraid that he might be knocking on their school door the next morning, accompanied by his usual posse of photographers, cracking a horsewhip and shouting, "Chant your tables, you swine".

I tried to reassure them that, if you want to be Prime Minister, you don't harangue your party conference about the virtues of progressive primary education. Tell them you will restore capital punishment for teachers who don't set daily spelling tests and a standing ovation is assured. Party conference time is a game with its own set of rules and conventions. The primary heads were still inconsolable.

It set me thinking about what a daft and over-simplified debate it had all become. The very word "traditional" immediately secures knee-jerk reactions. Mutter it to one group and a round of drinks will follow to toast solid British virtues such as industry, determination and thoroughness. Utter it in different company and the jeers will ring in your ears as people assume you are out of date, backward looking and embarrassed to the tips of your sensible shoes.

I reflected on a class of seven-year-olds I had been teaching. Had I been traditional or progressive, or, for that matter, did anyone give a hang? I had told them things, which sounds trad enough, but we had done a fair bit of group work, so perhaps I am a progressive. On the other hand, I had told some of the groups what to do, so I must be a traditional progressive, apart from when they are allowed to discuss the task I have set them with fellow pupils, because at these times I am a progressive traditional.

What the primary heads feared was that Mr Bun would try to import the styles of teaching he had seen in between posing for snapshots in the Soviet Union. It would not be so strange if Comrade Bunski had been over-impressed by the sort of primary school we used to have, in the 19th century, since therein lie the roots of his Education Act.

Just in case too much nostalgia for those awful days overwhelms us, perhaps we should recall some of their less happy features. Much of the time young children chanted by heart, slogans and epithets they ill-understood, like the capes and bays from Blackpool to Hong Kong when they knew neither what a cape nor a bay was. It made the "'ere we go, 'ere we go" equivalents of modern football crowds sound positively cerebral.

While he was in Russia Mr Bun did, of course, give his own exceptionally traditional lesson, which one journalist told me would have secured E-Minus on any teacher appraisal. It was shown on national television news when he was seen declaiming "The Charge of the Light Brigade" to an utterly poleaxed group of Russian teenagers.

My journalist friend tells me it was one of the rummest events he has seen in his cynical life. Apparently Bunski rushed into this room full of bewildered Russian students and produced, as if by magic, a class set of *Bun's Bumper Funbook of English Verse* which he just happened to have with him.

A hapless DES menial had lugged them across Siberia waiting for the right photo opportunity. He is probably now in hospital suffering from double hernia. It was as if Gorbachev had descended on some unsuspecting GCSE class at Little Piddlington Comprehensive, put on a record of *Gorby's Greatest Hits* and proceeded to do a Cossack dance for the assembled press.

Suddenly this crazy stranger with the manic smile and glinting glasses was ranting on about a battle at which 600 rode into the valley of death. Here was the embarrassing situation of a son of the nation which, during the Crimean War, sent the Light Cavalry Brigade on one of the most futile charges in military history, reading a poem about it to the descendents of those who had slaughtered them. It had all the ingredients of the bad trad lesson, the oblivious preaching to the uncomprehending.

So why had Bun suddenly gone a bundle on resurrecting what was condemned as a failure by successive 19th century critics? Listen carefully to the words of his poem and all becomes clear. Canon to the left of him, Canon to the right of him. There were also a few Nikons, Leicas and Sony television cameras back and front.

Going cheap at £7 million

Psssst...wanna buy a city technology college, cheap? Come over here. Look lady, don't walk away, come here a minute. Normally you have to raise a few million quid from industry, right? But to you let's call it half price, now what could be fairer? All right then, I'll tell you what, I like your face. I've gone stark staring mad, I'm giving them away today. The missus'll kill me when I get home. I'm not offering you £3 million, not four, not five, not six even. Special price to you and for today only, I'll give you £7 million towards your CTC. Now be fair, that's more than I'm spending on the whole county.

Despite the huckster style of market selling, there has not been too much success on the CTC front since it was given pride of place in the 1988 Education Act amid great fanfares. There were originally supposed to be 20 in operation by the end of the decade, a number which is already looking poorly.

Indeed, Bob Dunn, former education junior minister, once said there would be 120, 220, 320, even 420, and he would no doubt have gone higher had he not run out of fingers. In reality only modest progress has been made, and without Cyril Taylor, the man who has raised such cash and sites as have materialized, the whole idea would have been an even more monumental flop.

Consequently more than a touch of desperation has been apparent from the moment Mr Bun's travelling media circus descended on the first CTC when it opened in Solihull, bristling with microcomputers. Calling the register? Use a microcomputer. Somewhere to put your coffee? Stand it on the nearest microcomputer. Itchy back? Scratch it on the microcomputer. There were hi-tech solutions everywhere.

Millions of pounds of government rather than sponsorship cash have had to be pumped in to save face, and the latest wheezes strain credulity even more. The idea of creating commercially-sponsored technology colleges has receded. The response has been either apathy, or in most cases downright hostility. Many idustrialists, thankfully, are much keener to carry on supporting their local schools than finance a new artificially well resourced rival, knowing what harm it will do to carefully-conceived plans.

In the wake of these setbacks all kinds of remedies are being sought. Recently an increasingly desperate Singalong a Bun announced a city show-biz college financed by pop stars and record companies. There is a talk of a church of England CTC. As Robin might well have said to his partner in these circumstances, "Holy Technology, Batman, the Joker's back in Gotham City".

There must be more possibilities. How about a city mortuary attendants' college, presumably in the dead centre of town? I must try and establish a city estate agents' college. The advantage of this would be that when we operate from a cramped attic with three books and a couple of dubious "licensed teachers", the brochure would read: "Compact and cosy premises in bijou desirable residence with well established traditional learning resources and Government-approved expert teaching."

If all the rumours about Mr Bun moving to the Home Office are true, we can also have a city safecrackers' college. Perhaps there will be tests for policemen at 7,11,14 and 16 o'clock, opted-out prisons, a national BBC curriculum and Baker Days for convicts (the screws are sent home and the cons discuss whose turn it is to use the prison pencil).

The CTC idea could even be exported where it might be better appreciated. I recently spent a day in Madrid where the Spanish Minister of Education had invited me to advise him about the reorganisation of Spanish education. Before the sessions began the two translators were keen to discuss any words or phrases which might not be easy to translate.

We went through "city technology college", "community school", "tertiary college" until we ran into a snag. I wanted to explain that, although I was very enthusiastic about much of what I would describe and suggest, there were certain developments about which I was less than ecstatic. Indeed, I pointed out, I had been a bit critical of our own Minister.

Jokes rarely work in another language, and though "Baker" was no problem, translating "Mr Bun" caused furrowed brows. There was no real equivalent to "bun", I was told, but *"bunuelo"* might do. Fair enough, Senor Bunuelo it is. Ah, came the reply, this would not be a good translation because a Spanish bun was not quite the same as an English bun. Ever more curious I asked why. "Well, you see," the translator replied, "a Spanish bun looks very nice on the outside but it is hollow in the middle." *Olé* squire.

Bringing a Martian down to Earth

Dear Zarg,

It was good to receive your annual letter asking for an update on British education for your anthropological guide to the solar system. As you are the only Martian I know, other than the one who works at the Department of Education and Science writing circulars to schools, I am grateful to you for keeping me up to date on what is happening on other planets and only too happy to answer the many questions in your letter.

You mention the radio programme you heard indistinctly in which someone purporting to be a Government minister said that there was no shortage of teachers and that morale was sky high. You ask if this was a radio play about life earlier this century, or whether it is an example of what we Earth people call "optimism."

The distinction may be hard for you to follow, but it was not a radio play, though it was a piece of fiction, and "optimism" is only one of a number of Earth words that might be used to describe it. I am afraid I cannot answer your other queries about whether or not there are fairies at the bottom of the Minister's garden and if pigs can fly.

There is indeed a paradox, as you point out, in the same Ministers who deny any problems in teacher supply being frantic to enlist teachers from other countries. I think you have confused two quite different news stories when you ask why the Minister is recruiting Great Danes and Rottweilers. This has nothing to do with the Government's policy on school discipline. The Minister has been trying to persuade teachers in Denmark and Germany to come and teach in Britain, so your question about whether or not dogs are being recruited as licensed teachers does not apply, though those that can do tens and units will have a sporting chance.

I had not realised that there was such a teacher shortage on Venus that teachers had to be brought in from Mercury and that they were paid huge transfer fees. You ask whether the teachers from Hong Kong who answer the Government's appeal will be paid a transfer fee or need to have £150,000 in their bank account, in accordance with likely policy towards others granted a full British passport.

I do not know the answer to this, nor to your other question about why teachers are not offered higher salaries in Britain to encourage more people into the profession. Incidentally teachers are not being given food rather than money. When you heard they were paid "peanuts", this was not to be taken literally, though it is probably only a matter of time.

You are right to express concern, by the way, at the circular your Martian colleague at the DES has just sent round to schools about how much time is being spent on each topic in the national curriculum. I too have read this circular. The reason it has that page of what you call " pure gemstones" at the front with clarifications like, "The term '1988 Act' refers to the 1988 Education Reform Act" is, as you suspect, to help all those imported German teachers who might have thought it was the 1988 Road Traffic or Sewage Act.

I was not aware that someone who wrote a similar circular on Jupiter was sent to Neptune for it, but I share your anxiety about asking schools who do topics like "volcanoes" or "our village" to fill in hundreds of little squares saying how many hours and minutes of it were mathematics, geography or music. It does not mean that teachers will actually have to sing the national curriculum, as I gather they do on Uranus, but your expression "unnecessary bureaucratic bull dung" is near enough to the usual Earth term.

Finally I greatly enjoyed your interpretation of several news stories. I had indeed spotted the national newspaper adverts for the first British astronaut. It is quite true that the person chosen would have to go to Moscow and learn Russian. I had not realised, until you pointed it out, however, that it solved the mystery about Kenneth Baker's political future.

It was all so obvious, when you explained it. The project is being sponsored by television companies, so there will be plenty of photo opportunities, and he will be able to declaim in outer space *The Charge of the Light Brigade,* and other poems from his bumper funbook of English verse, to his fellow students.

It was your last observation, however, which made it so brilliant, when you revealed that he had already made appointments on other planets, to recruit Martian, Venusian and Neptunian teachers as he slicks his way across the galaxy. *"Vorsprung Durch Brylcreem"* as they say on Pluto. Have a good summer.

How the timetables have turned

Since the publication of the major report on the three core subjects of the national curriculum, mathematics, science and English, two words have been on the lips of the nation's teachers: "Tee hee". What started off as an exercise in bashing current practice in schools has turned out to be an endorsement of it. So the Cox Report on English for 5 to 11 year-olds, far from turning the clock back to the 19th century, has produced a sane account which commends the best of what has been achieved in the 20th.

Laugh? I haven't chortled so much since I found out that Kenneth Baker's middle name was Wilfred. That, incidentally, was only hilarious because the Wilfred I knew in my childhood was Wilf the local yokel, a toothless gaffer whose image was a million miles adrift from the one Wilf the Bun seeks for himself.

The rhythm of these committees on subject content and, indeed, on such matters as testing, has followed a remarkably consistent pattern. It will be interesting to see if this is maintained when all the other subject groups have been set up. Take the imaginary national curriculum subject of alchemy, which would have made it on to the list had its popularity not waned by the 19th century.

First, Wilf sets up the Alchemy Committee having vetted possible candidates. The committee is, on the surface, 'safe", but not as right-wing as the press sometimes makes out. For example, Professor Jason Headbanger, director of alchemy at Rotherham University, author of the book *Alchemy in schools has now been taken over by left-wing trendies: an objective appraisal,* is not a member.

Nor is Sir Herbert Mettle, managing director of Mettlesome School Canes, who knows nothing about alchemy but believes all teachers should be horsewhipped. The Prime Minister was in favour of him, but since she had already vetoed Alice Reasonable, head of alchemy at Swinesville comprehensive, for having once contemplated joining the NUT, she has "given way", the press tells us, to the wishes of Wilf.

About half way through the committee's deliberations one member resigns and there are rumours of a rift between the chair of the group and Wilf. When the report is published it is, contrary to the Government's expectation, in favour of much current practice and is welcomed by the teaching unions. Worse, and this really sticks in Wilf's craw, it is received with enthusiasm by the National Association of Teachers of Alchemy, so there must be something wrong with it.

The press now reveals that the Prime Minister is not happy with the report so Wilf tapes his smile to his head and goes on television to say that, while he in general welcomes the report, he is concerned that it neglects basic alchemy, whatever that may be.

At this point he may have a row with the Alchemy Committee Chair. He may actually swear at him, saying "you will bloody well do what you were asked to do," not nice, but an interesting use of the embellished adverb. I am afraid Wilf does browbeat his own officials that way as well. They do not like it, and it is at odds with his image.

Nevertheless, if we are to be rescued from the awfulness of what the national curriculum might have been, then I could not be happier. At least we seem likely to get a framework which allows teachers to teach in an enlightened way. The next "Tee hee", by the way, will come when someone adds up the consequences for the whole curriculum of each subject committee claiming 10 or 20 per cent for itself. It will add up to 200 per cent of the week.

In the meantime, just contemplate the dreadful outcome of an English curriculum dominated by grammar grinding. It would have produced more examples like this little belter: "References to a public examination (including a prescribed public examination) are references to such an examination as it applies in relation to persons entered for any syllabus for that examination with a view to meeting the examination requirements for that syllabus so as to qualify for assessment for the purposes of determining their achievements in that examination on any particular occasion in any year when an assessment for the purposes of determining the achievements of persons entered for that examination takes place."

I have no idea what it means, and it is the sort of prose that gets crap a bad name. Where does it come from? A document dripping with countless examples of the utter deadness of language dominated by structure rather than the need for clarity and any sense of audience. It is an extract from Section 118 of Wilf's Education Act.

Best of Times, Worst of Times

Monday July 22, 1839

It is bad enough trying to teach in a voluntary school in these cruel hard times without the daily assault on my ears from that oleaginous fellow who drives the hackney carriage in which I travel to my employment each day. Ever since the Whig Government voted that Parliament should donate £20,000 to public education in 1832 I have been hopeful that conditions would improve.

Alas, these seven years have passed and we still have no new building, for these monies cannot be spent on anything else. Every time I describe, on my journey to school, the inequities in modern education, my carriage driver heaps scorn upon my protests. His name is Bunne, to be correct Kenneth Bunne, formerly a Baker before he forsook that calling to drive a hackney carriage, in preparation, as he would put it, for a career in politics.

His endless prattle wearies me... "Teachers, governor? I'd string them all up...Hanging's too good for them...I had that Lord Melbourne in the back of my cabriolet once". There is no end to his tedious and banal homespun philosophies, for which he craves an audience, and, in me, has found a captive one each morning and evening.

Tuesday

Good news, I do believe. Lord Melbourne's Government has, by means of an order in council, increased to £39,000 the sum to be spent on public education. A Committee of Council on Education is to be established with a view to creating a national system of education. One intention is to found a state normal school, a training college for elementary school teachers.

I am overjoyed at the prospect, though I fear the religious question may complicate matters. I understand that there will be three conditions attached to any money which may be disbursed for school buildings. First the structure of the school must be kept in good repair, second it must be open to inspection, but third, and this is the source of my joy, there must be trusts established which guarantee the education of children from poor families.

I cannot conceal my happiness as I ride in to the school, eager to share the good tidings with the children, proclaiming to Bunne that future generations will see this year of 1839, which began so unpromisingly, as a turning point in the history of English education. Predictably, the unctuous fellow dampens my enthusiasm with his own vision of the future. Were he charged with responsibility for public education, a thought which chills me to the marrow, he would treat each school as a business, he tells me. Those that made a profit would flourish, those that made a loss could perish. This he justifies on the grounds that this philosophy worked admirably in the market where he used to sell loaves when he was a Baker.

Wednesday

There is more good news. The Government is to introduce next year a Bill into Parliament which will redirect many ancient endowments of the grammar schools into elementary schools. Much of this money has been wasted on poor quality classical education and I am convinced that we in the elementary schools could spend it more efficaciously.

Furthermore, the Government will facilitate the conveyancing of land to parishes which seek to build a new school. Many of the landed gentry are said to be prepared to act as benefactors with speed and generosity. It does begin to look more propitious, almost as if public education could be established through several such initiatives, rather than just one.

Even this does not please Bunne. During my ride home he relates at length his own proposals. The very giving of funds, he argues, would make schoolmasters indolent. What is more, he prates, warming to his task, the children would also become idle if schools and schooling were freely provided from the public purse. They ought, in any case, to be given stringent tests by the age of seven at the latest. Indeed his friend Boy Son believes that pupils must be severely chastised should they make errors in such tests. My argument that returning to the rough practices of the 18th century would be undesirable falls on stony ground.

Thursday

Bunne will sometimes make strange claims during our journeys. His most recent is that he has had audiences with Her Majesty the Queen and is privy to her thoughts on the education of her subjects. The Queen has only been on the throne for two years. of course, and it was my impression that she was completely under the influence of Melbourne, but Bunne claims she has confided in him her disappointment at the ignorance of her subjects. She seeks to have a set of values attached to her name and Bunne asserts that he will one day be charged with implementing them. This cannot entirely be true, because others swear that he was given a liberal thrashing with her handbag on the one occasion when he offered an opinion.

Nevertheless, when I proposed the essentials of what, in my opinion, should be taught to young children, Bunne dissented, propounding that he was much impressed with what Napoleon had achieved in France, and would himself, given the chance, prescribe exactly what every child in England should learn. I confirmed my gratitude that he drove a hackney carriage rather than directed the learning of Her Majesty's subjects, but he is unabashed by any contrary opinion. Indeed he has written to the author Charles Dickens, telling of his admiration for his new novel *Oliver Twist* which was published last year. He seeks to know if the character of Fagin was based on any real person as he would want such a person to advise him on teaching methods and the place of private enterprise in competition with public educational provision.

Friday

I fear Bunne's fantasies are becoming the better of him. His latest is that he has secured access to a time machine which will propel him 150 years into the future. Such is his hostility to the birth of public education, he tells me as we drive home from school, that, unable to prevent its genesis he must travel ahead in time and suffocate its future. Once he has begun the decline of publicly funded education, according to the plan he has conceived, he will then eliminate it completely by winning first the post of Conservative Party chairman and later that of Prime Minister. I cannot for one moment believe, as he avers, that he will not be driving me to school next Monday as he will have transported himself into the late 20th century, the year 1989 if my arithmetic is correct. In any case by that time public education would surely have become so securely established that even the demented Bunne could not dismantle it. The very idea is preposterous, is it not?

Master Wragg

A welcome change of voice

When John MacGregor, recently appointed Secretary of State for Education, went to Cambridgeshire to address his first meeting of head teachers at the beginning of this month, two unusual events took place: first he announced he was actually going to stop something happening, rather than introduce yet more changes, and secondly he told the heads he wanted to listen to their views. His speech signalled a turning point in education.

His announcement that the teacher appraisal scheme would be delayed was cheered, not out of hostility, but because it was eroding the time needed to do everything else; nobody could remember when a minister had last received such warm approval from the teaching profession. After a decade which had seen four major Education Acts — in 1980, 1981, 1986 and the biggest of all in 1988 — as well as the introduction of new examinations like the GCSE, the change of style could not have been more welcome.

It was the sharp acceleration in the rate of reform under Kenneth Baker that fuelled many of the problems of the past two years. The 1988 Education Act introduced a national curriculum with a compulsory new syllabus for each of 10 subjects, national assessment for children at the ages of seven, 11, 14 and 16, and new kinds of school to compete with the maintained sector, like the City Technology Colleges and the Grant Maintained Schools which had opted out of local authority control. In addition, schools were to manage their own finances and governing bodies were given increased power.

The contrast between MacGregor and his predecessor was stark. Under Baker, teachers had felt they were being used by a media-hungry ambitious politician to further his own career. Even minor amendments or innovations were given heavy publicity as part of his "wheeze-a-week" style. In order to justify the need for change, Baker overplayed criticism of the profession, leading to a drop in morale and serious recruiting problems. Worried senior civil servants made no secret of their attempts to persuade ministers to be more encouraging to teachers.

It was significant, therefore, that MacGregor emphasized his wish to listen in his Cambridgeshire speech, saying "I am a listener as well as a decision-maker" and "I think the Government sometimes sets too short a period for consultative processes and I am very conscious of your present workload". He had clearly become aware of the hostility generated when Baker launched the consultation exercise on the introduction of a national curriculum in late July 1987. Replies were expected by the beginning of September, giving just the month of August for a response to one of the most significant changes ever undertaken in education.

The skills of good management include giving respect to and in turn earning it from, the workforce, the ability to discriminate between necessary and unnecessary change, and an awareness that, if overload has occurred, alleviating action must be taken. Whereas Baker failed to grasp these basic principles, MacGregor seems eager to embrace them.

So far, he has knocked two green bottles off the wall. The delay in the implementation of teacher appraisal was one welcome source of relief to heads in particular. Of greater political significance, however, was his announcement that no more public money would be put into City Technology Colleges. It was noteworthy that MacGregor made his keynote speech to a meeting of head teachers. They are the main lever pullers in the educational system.

If he listens to heads, he will hear they are overwhelmed by petty bureaucracy, with silly forms to fill in about which bits of the national curriculum they have taught and for how long. MacGregor's moves may have considerable influence beyond the education service. There is a close parallel between education and other public services such as health. The aggravation between doctors and ministers is very similar to that between teachers and ministers some 18 months ago. His quiet role sweeping up bottles after the party is over will be watched with interest for the significance it may one day have elsewhere.

Chapter 2

Mad Curriculum Disease

In search of a true explorer

It did take a very long time for the membership of the national curriculum geography committee to be announced. The reason for this delay, I am told, was that Mr Bun wanted an explorer to chair it, but could not find one.

Now this does raise several very interesting issues, not the least of which is that it is hardly surprising that Bun could not turn up a real live explorer. If there is one human group that is not sitting in an armchair clutching a mug of hot cocoa, waiting for Bun to phone, it is the genus explorers. It ought to have been screamingly obvious that real explorers are out exploring, so head for the North Pole if you want one.

The thought of Bun wading neck deep up the Limpopo, complete with pith helmet, pursued by a dozen camera crews, cracked me up: "Dr Livingstone, I presume, would you like to chair my geography committee?" Perhaps he disguised himself as Kenneth "the Eagle" Baker in the last winter Olympics in the faint hope of finding a curriculum minded explorer up in the Arctic wastes. I suppose we are lucky the geography committee is not being chaired by some bewildered Eskimo.

The main question it raised for me, however, was about the nature of professionalism. There is a tendency nowadays for some politicians to assume that people professionally involved in an enterprise are not capable of considering wider issues, belong to a self-protecting interest group, cannot empathize with the non-expert, and are incapable of objective judgement. Yet many true experts have none of these faults, even if some do, and it is wrong to assume that an amateur is always needed for wise decisions to be reached.

Another aspect of professionalism under threat in education is over the matter of school support services.

Though usually referred to as "jobs" rather than "professions", occupations such as school caretaker, secretary, cleaner and so on have often been carried out according to the best tenets of professionalism, with complete commitment to the school community.

The provision of contracted privatized service could offer a cheaper and more efficient service to schools once they have local financial management and are able to choose their supplier. It might also, I fear, jeopardize that dedicated commitment by on-site caretakers and cleaners, who have often built up over many years that strong sense of devotion to duty which is a hallmark of good professionalism.

In one area which has already set up such a service the dangers are clear to see. Caretakers have been given cars, mobile phones, a written contract and several schools to patrol. Newly Yuppified they cruise round the country-side opening the first schools on their list as early as six am on the grounds that the contract only says "unlock the schools", it doesn't say at what time. When a pupil is sick in a classroom and the head rings up Alpha Delta Four on his mobile phone, the reply comes that there is nothing about cleaning up vomit in the contract. Consequently heads and teachers are mopping up, cleaning out swimming pools and doing several jobs formerly undertaken without demur by their local on-site caretaker.

If there is one notion, however, which chills the blood so far as profes-sionalism is concerned, it is that of "awareness". There is so much for teachers to cover nowadays that the universal answer is the "awareness" course. Next time a surgeon advances towards you in quest of your appendix ask him whether he has been on an awareness course or actually knows what he is doing.

I remember taking part in a long ashen-faced discussion a few years ago when special educational needs became a buzzword. Should we put on courses for specialists so that they could become trainers of their colleagues, or ought we to mount awareness courses for those who confessed ignorance? We preferred the trainers' course, but the local authority wanted an awareness course. We called it a "training awareness" course to please everyone.

The themes for awareness rain down: the demands of the 1988 Act, plus the need to be aware of the powers of governing bodies, the views of employers. Teachers wake up in the middle of the night shouting "Leave me alone. I'm aware, I'm aware".

I watched a news item on television about an education train that cruises round Wales taking children out on field trips. It was a brilliant idea. We could use it for awareness courses: "The 10:15 awareness train is about to depart on platform six, calling at special needs, pupil assessment, swimming pool maintenance, cleaning up litter, and all stops to local financial management." The train driver could go on to chair the national curriculum geography committee.

A ghost still full of beans

One of my greatest pleasures, as a youth, was to act in the school play. We would stay on after school and live through some monumental drama, week upon week, until we all knew every word off by heart, irrespective of the part we were playing. To this day I can recall the chilling experience of seeing Macbeth confronted by the ghost of Banquo. I was reminded a couple of weeks ago of how the poor beggar must have felt, watching someone he thought had passed on actually appear before his eyes.

There I was, innocently watching the news, barely sober after a six week celebration at Mr Bun having finally departed from the DES, leaving only the faintest whiff of scorched Brylcreem, the first, and hopefully last holo- gram to be Education Secretary, when Old Smarmy Boots rushed before the cameras in the yard of the first opted-out school. It was only catatonic shock that prevented me leaping up and declaiming like the demented Macbeth, "Hence horrible shadow! Unreal mockery, hence!"

Not that I am opposed to these photo-opportunities, you understand. After all, it was an everyday occurrence at my school for us to stroll across the playground holding hands with a Cabinet Minister and the headmaster wearing his gown, and smiling at the assembled press. What shocked me was the thought that Bun might go on appearing in school yards and classrooms to the end of time, gibbering on about the success of his Education Act. Perhaps in 50 years' time the BBC will be cashing in on the nostalgia for it with *Dad's Army,* the story of a few intrepid, if comical, elderly licensed teachers, and *'Allo 'Allo,* a series about teachers imported from France trying to control 3C on a wet Friday afternoon.

It was no surprise to discover that one of Bun's first moves as Conservative Party chairman was to hire the marketing firm which had been responsible for relaunching a well-known brand of baked beans, to revamp the Govern- ment's image. I always thought his style was more suited to selling beans than nurturing the nation's youth. Apparently his and their first job is to find a new logo for the Government, to replace the torch symbol they nicked from the National Union of Teachers, a few years ago. I suggest a great big bean.

It would commemorate Bun's mercifully brief sojourn in education and the flatulence that accompanied it, and he would go down in history as Bun the Bean.

Most of the subject reports for the national curriculum which have appeared so far seem to incorporate some of the best classroom practice of recent years. My worry, like that of other teachers, is that there has not been enough time to plan, that the money for all the necessary resources may not be provided, and that the demands of testing and the sheer volume of cumulative requirements might between them screw the whole thing up. I am already getting a bit neurotic, with any class I teach, about which of the attainment targets I might have covered.

Last week I was playing a game with a class of five-year-olds who had just started school. They had to point to their eyes, their nose or whatever, when I mentioned these, and then they could move to "Cleverland". Normally it would have been the sort of harmless game one plays with children of five without further ado, but this time it was a special occasion. I had just "delivered" my first piece of the national curriculum, science national curriculum attainment target three, "Processes of Life", level one, ("know parts of the body"), to be precise. Only 9,999 to go, or rather "be delivered", must keep up the beans jargon.

It occurred to me that there could be an economical, (or is it "cost effective"?) way of delivering the beans, as they no doubt say in Bun's office nowadays. What I needed was a single inspiration, some monumentally comprehensive but brief event, which would wipe out the whole of the primary national curriculum in one fell swoop. Suddenly I had it. All we needed to do was sing my old childhood favourite. *The Grand Old Duke of York*. It was brilliant and will save me hours.

Since it is a poem, that covers English, and if you sing it as well then you have taken care of music. The rest of the national curriculum goes like this.

Oh, the Grand Old Duke of York.
(history)
He had 10,000 men;
(maths)
He marched them up to the top of the hill,
Then he marched them down again
(PE and geography)
And when they were up they were up,
And when they were down they were down)
(Science, — well, it included "measurement and observation")

And when they were only half-way up,
They were neither up nor down.

The relevance of this last couplet may be obscure but I am calling it design and technology on the grounds that business studies is subsumed under the design-and-technology heading and the two lines sum up beautifully the state of many British businesses. If you are in any doubt you can always get the class to type the poem on the word processor and then log it in under the information technology attainment target of the design-and-technology label.

The children then paint a picture of it, so that takes care of art, and all nine subjects are under your belt. Secondary teachers can ask the class to translate it into French, thus nailing modern languages at the same time. So there you are, the whole national curriculum in just a single lesson. It's the absolute beans.

Life, the universe and toenail clipping

If you are planning to win the BBC's annual *Mastermind* competition during the 1990s, then my advice to you is this: become a primary teacher. The latest manifestation of Mad Curriculum Disease, namely the publication of the Plato to NATO history report, confirms that, when all the national curriculum subject syllabuses are available, the amount of knowledge primary teachers are expected to possess will be colossal.

Picture the scene. It is the 1995 *Mastermind* final. Fresh from imbibing the, by now, 73 science attainment targets, you are called into the famous black chair.

"*Your name?*" enquires Magnus.
"Mavis Clutterbuck"
"*Your occupation?*"
"Primary school teacher"
"*And your chosen subject?*"

Deep breath, "Every conceivable damned thing about every possible subject from the beginning of time to the expiry of the Universe and beyond".

I've started, so I'll finish (as the Prime Minister remarked when she had dragged the interim report of the history working party half way through the shredder). The sheer volume of knowledge primary teachers are now required to master takes the breath away. In the science curriculum there are topics like genetics, electricity and magnetism, earth sciences, climatology, and in technology children must learn to design prototypes, build a functioning machine, and use appropriate materials, components, processes and techniques in a wide range of manufacturing activities.

The publication of the history proposals makes the story even worse. The result of countless hands on the tiller, including those of Miss Piggy herself, is an overfull bag of topics from the ancient Egyptians to the present day. Whereas the English proposals refrained from prescribing in detail such matters as the books or authors children should be required to read, there is no reluctance to be prescriptive in the history report. It is awash with what is called essential and exemplary information.

Although exemplary information is only for guidance, the report makes it clear that "essential" information must be taught by law. In future primary teachers will actually be lawbreakers if they fail to teach a list of some 129 prescribed sub-topics in the core and optional themes. Let me just mention but a tiny fraction of the topics from the core subjects alone that teachers will be legally required to cover: Boudicca, Celtic Christianity, Anglo-Saxon pagan artefacts, Norse sagas, Isaac Newton, public health and nutrition in Victorian Britain, unemployment in the 1930s, the building technology used for the pyramids and the Parthenon, Egyptian agriculture, the medieval trade in spices, and Aztec religion.

The legally required factual content of the six optional topics includes such belters as:the technology of oar power, food production in Neolithic times, 18-century changes in husbandry, Gutenberg and early printing, transport before and after the wheel (I'm not making these up, honest), draught animals and changes in plough design. How the committee left out such essentials as toenail clipping in ancient Babylon, bee symbolism in medieval literature and the evolution of the nose flute, is beyond me.

What on earth are they going to do with teachers who do not or cannot cover these vast lists of legally compulsory facts, gaol them?

But your Honour, I had to spend so much time on my PhD in physics to cope with the science curriculum, I never had time to read up on Aztec strangling rituals.

"Prison's too good for the likes of you, Mrs Clutterbuck. It is my duty to protect society from teachers who don't know their Aztecs from their Elgar. You will spend the rest of your natural life reading every single national curriculum document twice." Gasps from relatives in the public gallery.

All this detailed prescription makes a mockery of the assurance by John MacGregor's predecessor, whose name escapes me, that the national curriculum would be a framework not a straitjacket. What legally required goodies will future reports contain? Will the PE report demand pole vaulting and pelota, and the music curriculum prescribe heavy gaol sentences for those who fail to teach children the cello and saxophone?

There are further sinister developments. Normally public response to final reports has been solicited by the National Curriculum Council, but reaction to the history report has to be sent to the Schools Branch of the Department of Education and Science itself, confirming the increasingly tight and repressive Government control of the whole exercise. Presumably you begin your reply "Dear Branch", or "Dear Schools" if you prefer the informality of Christian names.

I was, until recently, at a loss to explain this prescriptive fact-laden approach to learning. After all, Mr MacGregor himself said publicly that the Battle of Trafalgar was in 1815 instead of 1805, giving rise, no doubt, to the new saying, "He's met his Trafalgar", meaning the penultimate rather than ultimate cropper. Another Government minister, to his embarrassment, could not give the date of Wat Tyler's rebellion on the BBC's *Question Time*.

Why, I have been asking myself, are schools being sent these thick 200-plus page, detail-packed documents for every subject under the sun? What is the purpose of mailing sack after sack of the wretched things to every school in the land? Then I realised that there was indeed a supreme master plan, so brace yourself. The revelation I am about to make is sensational.

You may have noticed that the documents are getting thicker and thicker, but that they are still in the same A4 format. I can now reveal that they are in fact not curriculum documents at all, *but rather parts of a super gun.* I have had this confirmed by Customs and Excise, who immediately banned the export of any more national curriculum documents in case they should fall into the hands of an unfriendly foreign power.

If you roll each document into a cylindrical shape and then glue them all together they make a huge super gun. When all the reports are out, every school will be sent a piece of long thin wire and a large sachet of gunpowder. Then, in fulfilment of attainment target 3 of the design and technology curriculum (make an artefact, system or environment), 27,000 primary and secondary schools will wire their super guns together.

Finally the Prime Minister, who has belatedly, it appears, discovered that the curriculum is a mite overcrowded, will press a detonator, and BOOM! 27,000 loads of bureaucratic bullshit are simultaneously blasted into outer space, puncturing an almight hole in the ozone layer, and thereby ensuring mild winters and warm summers for the rest of the century. Brilliant.

A Trojan horse designed by committee

When the 1988 Education Act established a national curriculum of 10 subjects to be taught in all state schools, few tipped history to be what sports commentators call "the Big One". Yet last week's final report of the Government working party on school history brought combatants swarming on to the battlefield like the great armies about which they were arguing.

The content of each national curriculum subject is drawn up by a specialist working party, which makes recommendations to the Secretary of State. History was the fifth of the 10 subjects to reach the final report stage. Mathematics, science, English and technology had entered the statute books with barely a murmur. The history working party, however, has been riven with controversy from the start.

It began with the choice of chairman. Politically ambitious Kenneth Baker was keen to appoint a chairman who might catch the public eye. He tried to find an explorer to chair the geography committee, for example, but most were, understandably, somewhere up the Limpopo. The chairman of the history working party, Commander Michael Saunders Watson, was an unusual choice, since he was the owner of a stately home rather than a professional historian.

Next there were stories from candidates for the committee itself, telling how ministers had probed to see if they were sound on the teaching of historical facts rather than all this trendy stuff about empathising with medieval peasants. The actual meetings were conducted in greater secrecy than in other subjects. After they had produced their draft interim report a DES official went around emptying the wastepaper bins, presumably in case someone had doodled "Tudors and Stuarts" or "Ancient Greece" on a scrap of paper.

Trouble really began when the Prime Minister signalled her displeasure with the interim report last summer. Not enough emphasis on facts, nor sufficient British history, was her verdict. John MacGregor — newly arrived successor to Mr Baker — anxious, no doubt, to please his benefactress, agreed with her and asked the committee to think again.

I happened to meet the Prime Minister just after she had seen the interim report. "Have you seen those history proposals?" she raged in Miss Piggy mode. "*I don't like* them. *I don't like* them at all." I was tempted to ask her if, on balance, she was against them.

By contrast R A Butler, in his engaging autobiography, *The Art of the Possible,* tells how he was asked by Churchill to introduce more patriotism into schools. "Tell them that Wolfe won Quebec," said Churchill. Mr Butler relates: "I said that I would like to influence what was taught in schools but this was always frowned upon." Churchill accepted this, saying: "Of course, not by instruction or order, but by suggestion."

Last week's final report is a classic example of what happens when everyone's hand has been on the master plan. The result is an enormous Plato-to-Nato syllabus, packed with what is called "essential information", that is, facts that must be taught by statute, and "exemplary information", facts that are optional.

This has produced some interesting selections. Under modern American history Roosevelt and Martin Luther King are compulsory, but Kennedy, Pearl Harbour, McCarthyism and Vietnam are optional. In 20th century British-history Asquith and Lloyd George are compulsory, Ramsay MacDonald, Baldwin, Macmillan and Wilson are optional; most of the 1920s, the 1950s and the years post-1969 do not exist at all, though Russian-history goes right up to Gorbachev.

There is considerable dismay among teachers that they must, by statute, teach so many topics, some of which will be relatively unfamiliar to them. Primary teachers in particular have expressed concern that they will be lawbreakers if they fail to teach seven-to-11-year-olds about Boudicca, King Alfred, Norse sagas, Celtic Christianity, Cromwell, Newton, Queen Victoria, unemployment in the 1930s, the technology of the Pyramids and the Parthenon, Aztec religion and the route to the Spice Islands.

That is less than a quarter of the legally "essential" topics that all junior school pupils must cover. There are more statutory requirements under options such as "food and farming", "ships and seafarers" or "writing and printing", and a spell in jug awaits those primary teachers who fail to mention changes in plough design, the technology of oar power, Gutenberg and 58 other required bits of information.

The syllabus for secondary pupils is equally overcrowded. (In an optional unit on the British Empire, the 1877 to 1905 maps with all the red bits on are legally required, so this ought to placate some critics.)

One of the complicating features of the history syllabus is that it is written under four headings. Every single topic or period has, in effect, four related syllabuses: political; economic, technological and scientific; social and religious; cultural and aesthetic, or PESC as the report calls them after initials. Thus when younger secondary pupils study Islamic civilisation up to the 16th century they will cover the Ottoman Empire (political); the pepper trade (economic); the prophet Mohammed (social and religious); and Islamic architecture (cultural).

Yet if the range is commendable, there are too many features that seem bizarre because they are the preferences of one small group. Why, for example, is the 1914-1918 War optional when it has often been one of the most effectively taught topics in secondary schools? Why is the Second World War a statutory "essential" theme, but the rise of Hitler an optional "exemplary" one? Why on earth is the Labour victory in 1945 down as a "social and religious" theme rather than a "political" one? Was someone praying for it?

The great pity is that the report has several good proposals that would have attracted widespread support, but it has gone over the top in its prescriptiveness and sheer volume.

The simplest level of the history syllabus is for five to-seven- year-olds, where work is built around such questions as "who am I?" and "where am I?" Those may well be the questions that their teachers will be asking themselves when the 10 increasingly fact-laden subjects of the national curriculum have been fully accepted.

Time for a fling with the cabinet

The language and artefacts of education nowadays never cease to amaze me. I suppose I should have become inured, but it goes way beyond the customary exhortation to "deliver" the curriculum or "market" the school. Some of the expressions used and the gear being dreamed up simply blow the mind.

Perhaps it is always so and one never really thought about it. After all I remember being a bit startled the first time I heard someone banging on about how important it was to "stretch" bright pupils. I was left with a ludicrous image of some poor beggar suspended from the ceiling with weights tied to his legs, or of the head running round antique shops frantically trying to buy a second-hand rack. Perhaps it was yet another design and technology attainment target.

Then I once had a secretary who made the same typing errors over and over again. Her usual one was to catch one of the fraction keys a glancing blow, so that references would read, "Mr Simpkins is ½ good at keeping order and ½ enthusiastic about his work".

One of her better ones, however was to miss out an "i" in "filing cabinet". I got fed up of receiving notes asking what a "fling cabinet" was and what I could conceivably want to do with it. Perhaps every staffroom should have one so that teachers suffering from Mad Curriculum Disease could go inside and hurl themselves around for fun.

Another term that has crept on to the scene is the notion of "mapping" cross-curricular themes on to the national curriculum. Geographers threatened with redundancy could make a fortune here, because the ability to "map" — that is to do something you intended to do anyway, but pretend it is a vital part of the national curriculum — is becoming a highly valued skill. Whole careers are going to be made or broken on the ability to map.

This mapping business reminds me of Ken Dodd's joke book. The great man has, over the years, categorized his jokes into groups, each with a name.

Thus "woofers" are jokes which are guaranteed to get a belly laugh, even in Glasgow. In curriculum-theme mapping the equivalent of a "woofer" is those attainment target statements that can be made to cover almost any human activity. The best examples come in subjects such as English, where children must talk and write about different topics for different audiences. There is almost nothing you cannot do under that sort of heading — rob a bank, take off to the south of France, watch *Racing from Epsom* on television.

One primary school head told me recently that he was rung up by an inspector who intended to visit him that very afternoon to see how he was mapping themes on to the national curriculum.

Aware that the school had been blithely sailing along, with barely a thought about the niceties of mapping, he frantically grabbed his record sheets and, he claims, randomly ticked various attainment targets for each topic tackled that term. The inspector came that afternoon and congratulated him on what he described as a "model of its kind". I suppose it was.

The advertising columns of the press are already full of people claiming to be able to "deliver", "market", "map", translate Madcurriculumspeak into modern English, or sell you some amazing educational artefact. I was recently sent an advert from an outfit that markets bar codes for teachers doing national curriculum assessments. I always thought a bar code contained advice like "Don't spit in your neighbour's lager" or "Don't drop crisps on the taproom floor", but it is those little black lines normally found on cans of beans in supermarkets.

Apparently this firm will sell you wads of stick-on bar codes which are then read by a laser beam as the children leave the class, saving you the bother of filling in your mark book. According to the sales literature it even buzzes and beeps if more than six pupils go out of the room without a bar code on their work. I was convinced it was a spoof but I am told it is real. I wonder if it could be rigged to sound a hooter when an inspector comes in to look at your maps. Whatever next?

A couple of weeks ago I had another of those "this must be a spoof" experiences. I was rung up by someone from a television programme and asked if I would comment on the state of school buildings, oh, and by the way, there would be a short film first. Fine, no problem.

I sat in frozen horror as some primary children politely explained in the film the problems of having to be taught in a toilet. Other pupils kept coming in and out and it did pong a bit. Was it real? Was I awake? Or would someone suddenly announce that breakfast was ready and it was time to get up? It was real enough.

Finally, let me tell you the best education joke I have heard recently. I don't know whether it really is the best, but it made me laugh loudest, so here it is for you, me, John MacGregor and anyone else who desperately needs a giggle at the end of term.

One Monday morning a teacher arrives in the DES reception area and tells the man at the desk that he would like to see Kenneth Baker. The commissionaire duly explains that Kenneth Baker is no longer the Minister in charge and that he does not now work at the DES. The teacher thanks him and leaves.

The next morning the same teacher arrives in DES reception and again asks if he can see Kenneth Baker. Once more the man in reception tells him patiently that he cannot see Mr Baker because he no longer works there. Once more the teacher thanks him and leaves. Exactly the same happens on the following two mornings. By Friday the receptionist is going crazy. The teacher turns up yet again and asks if he can see Kenneth Baker. "Look, I've told you every single day this week", the commissionaire begins, sinews standing out and eyes bulging. "Just get this into your head once and for all. Kenneth Baker doesn't work here any more," he bawls, pounding his fist on his desk, "so why do you keep asking?"

"I just like to hear you say it," the teacher replies.

Have a good summer.

Dodgy licences for the disqualified

If there is one thing that has pleased me immensely in recent weeks it is the discovery that the "licensed teacher" scheme is going to be a monumental flop. Despite Government hype to the contrary, this squalid proposal to turn loose on the classrooms of Britain thousand of unqualified teachers, possessing nothing more than the odd A-level and a Diploma in Bean Growing, will soon fizzle out like a cheap firework.

Nationally there have been a magnificent 46 or so applications from individuals, and some of the local authority bids for the couple of million made available by the Government, are for vast sums of money to support tiny numbers. The wretched proposal will be unpopular, expensive and inefficient, in that it would be better to spend money training teachers properly, rather than sticking unqualified tyros straight into the classroom.

It is no use the Government arguing that the scheme must be a success, on the grounds that half the local authorities in the country have applied for support cash for licensed teachers. Such is the parlous state of LEA finances nowadays that the same would happen if you offered a couple of million to spend on toenail clippers. Never mind whether or not you need them, is the dictum, get your sticky fingers into the till, and then, with luck, you might be able to launder the loot into something more worthwhile.

My fevered imagination has been working overtime trying to see in what circumstances anyone would actually want a licensed teacher. I suspect it would be roughly as follows. North Swineshire Comprehensive finds itself in a bit of a dilemma with its design and technology department. Mr Cudworthy is teaching level 8 of attainment target 2 of the national curriculum in design and technology, which requires pupils to "experiment and take risks using familiar materials in unfamiliar ways or situations" when, in response to this challenge, 5F superglue him to the workshop ceiling. This finally persuades him it is time to leave the profession.

Mr Cudworthy is not the only member of the design and technology department who is leaving. Mrs Sanderson, the head of department, is going to work for Marks and Spencer, and Mr Bentley is taking early retirement, though only 29, claiming that, because he *feels* 65, he should be eligible to retire now.

That leaves just one member of staff in the department, who has sent the head a note which simply says, "As I am pregnant I shall be resigning as soon as possible". Since his name is Mr Jenkins, it is clear that he has become a trifle desperate to get out, hoping, as he puts it, to apply for a job which would be easier on the nerves, like poll-tax collector or kamikaze pilot.

The school duly advertises all four vacancies, stressing the tree-lined avenues of the North Swineshire Comprehensive campus, the happy staffroom atmosphere (though some teachers threaten to invoke the Trades Description Act on this one) even offering a 10 per cent discount on electrical goods, if purchased for cash, at the chairman of governors' SupaCheap out-of-town shopping mall, all to no avail.

Even the new school logo, which cost a cool £45,000, fails to pull them in, but then the head had warned the governors that, while a red Porsche with a gold cash register on the front seats made a certain symbolic impact on the business community, it would cut less ice in educational circles.

The one applicant is not a qualified teacher, but a 22-year-old German who, since leaving school, has worked for two years as a car-park attendant at the Mercedes factory in Stuttgart and has a Diploma in Advanced Multi-story Car Parking. The governors see the opportunity to take part in an exciting new Government scheme and appoint their first ever "licensed teacher", really putting the school on the map, so they interview him.

Colonel Ffrenchly-Fforbes, a governor who used to be in military intelligence, asks his standard Question, "Who won the FA Cup in 1937?"(Spies used to reply "Cologne United", worked every time). The chairman goes through the DES licensed teacher interview checklist — Has he got two heads? Is he on a life support machine? — that sort of thing.

Finally the governors decide that all Germans are highly industrious, technological whizz-kids who speak perfect English, so they offer him the job. When asked if he has any questions, he says, "Ja. Is it true zat ze places of learning in your country now ze nationalized curriculum hev?"

Many pressure groups have sought to get their favourite issue into the national curriculum: health education, citizenship, the environment, even the egg industry wanted eggological sciences. I was embarrassed to see, however, that the Family Planning Association has begun a campaign to make sex education a national curriculum subject.

Now don't misunderstand me. I am not against it. I am a broad- minded chap who is willing to have a go at teaching anything. On the same day I once taught science to a class of seven-year-olds, took a GCSE class in German, lectured to a group of undergraduates and held a PhD tutorial. But where sex education is concerned I am just not available. For me it has a squirm and cringe factor of 100.

For a start I am too ignorant. I have no idea whether caps and coils are things you put on your head or shove in your ear. Second, I am too bashful. I once watched a video of a sex education lesson which showed a teacher sliding a condom on to a banana. I just died. There are numerous thing I will do for Queen and country, but ramming a piece of fruit into a johnny in front of 4C and keeping a straight face is not one of them.

Does the Family Planning Association realise what it is letting us in for, I also ask myself. To take sex education under the national curriculum panoply is going much too far. What, for goodness' sake, will the attainment targets be? Worse, who will determine them? What will you have to do to be graded level 10 in bonking? And can you imagine administering standard assessment tasks? As Sam Goldwyn once said: include me out.

Suckers for snake oil hokum

If there is one element of this marketing mad world for which I have had not the smallest grain of sympathy, it is the quest for a corporate image. Commercial outfits are spending vast fortunes on logos, brand images, and choosing "house colours" as they are called.

The new chief executive of an international hotel chain once decided that their traditional colours of green and white were now dated. He made them change to the colours coffee and cream instead. Throughout the world hotel signs, sheets, towels, menu cards, letter heads were scrapped and replaced in the new house colours. Soon afterwards the next supremo made them all switch back to green and white.

All this cavorting and wasting of money in commerce would just be a hilarious aside were it not for the sad fact that education itself, still under the influence of Mr Bun, the supreme after-image, is falling for the hokum of the snake oil vendors. Frantically seeking that elusive corporate image, several institutions of higher education are spending in some cases sums of £30,000 to £50,000 for a logo. The ones I have seen so far include what looks like a broken chess piece, a line with a dot under it, a capital letter and a squashed fried egg.

All I can say is that I am available immediately to any university or polytechnic seeking such a logo. You want a capital letter? I'm your man. I have a choice of twenty-six available in a variety of colours. Anyone wishing to remain anonymous should just send the readies in used notes in a brown envelope, using the pseudonym "sucker" at this stage.

The bad news is that schools are under pressure to squander their hard earned cash on image-making. A few will no doubt scrap perfectly good school badges in favour of some ludicrously expensive and tasteless example of late 20th century commercial heraldry. Yet if there is one area where the reality is much more important than the image it is education.

I was wrong incidentally in guessing that Bun would choose a baked bean as the Tory Party's new logo. Instead it was again the torch rampant, but this time one that looked to be moving, with much more prominent licking flames, symbolic, presumably of his management of the education system and the fact that, having torched it, he ran like hell.

You can display a logo on the main street of Salzburg so long as it is made of wrought iron. Even the famous fast food hamburger joint was not allowed to have its customary red and yellow sign but had to settle for a wrought iron bun instead. I must remember to ask them to send one to Baker.

Recently two things happened which cheered me enormously about the complete dedication of teaching profession. The first was a report from the *Yorkshire Evening Post* about "the crazed gunman at the centre of a nation-wide police hunt".

Apparently this masked figure with a shotgun kidnapped an official of the National Union of Teachers, shutting him in the boot of his own car and driving off with him.

Could this have been Bun's last desperate act to solve the teacher shortages in some parts of the country by kidnapping citizens and then returning them as licensed teachers elsewhere? But the intrepid NUT man managed to escape and get back home. *The Yorkshire Evening Post* recorded for posterity the utter commitment of Britain's teachers: "He got help at the first house he came to and, when he arrived home, his teacher wife, who had been working at her desk, had not even noticed he had been missing". I bet the NUT man had been marking essays in the car boot as well.

Even more cheering was the discovery that the Prime Minister thinks teachers have done well with the GCSE. I actually got this one from the horse's mouth, if you'll forgive the expression, when I met her recently. Not that we often socialise, say at the supermarket checkout, or at the garden centre where she has her hair done. We don't go round together much, well, only rarely. All right, we've just met this once.

The experience reminded me of the quiz game question "Which famous person once came third in a Charlie Chaplin look-alike competition in Monte Carlo?" The answer is — Charlie Chaplin. Apparently the great man put on his gear, went along to the competition and really did come third. On meeting Miss Piggy, I wondered which of the impressionists had turned up. Full marks for the hair, but ring us again when you've got the voice right.

"What do you think of the GCSE?" she began, so I went into enthusiastic auto-pilot about "due reward for the sterling efforts of teachers and child-ren", "a real improvement not an artefact". Her response was a surprise: "Oh good, I'm so glad to hear it and I do so agree with you". So I took the opportunity to say she had been "a bit naughty" for blocking the proposed A-level reforms. "But we mustn't change you know", "Oh yes, we must".

Great fun this, especially as, unlike Bun, I did not have to dive under the table for fear of being fired or handbagged.

On the national curriculum history "Plato to NATO" syllabus she was more predictable: *"I don't like* the proposals, *I don't like* them, *I don't like* them at all"*. I resisted the temptation to reply: "So would you say, on balance, that you weren't in favour of them, then?"

Unfortunately I never got round to the spoof conversation I had dreamed up on my way to the tea party: "I say, I say, I say, Miss Piggy, do you know how to get children through the national curriculum in one third of the time?" "No, my good man, do tell me" "Microwave them". I meant to, but I forgot. Another CBE down the drain.

Getting to the heart of it

For those of us who love sport, taking games has always been a mixed blessing. On a fine sunny day with a keen group nothing could be finer. In pouring rain with reluctant conscripts most teachers can think of a better use of their time.

I once worked with a man who always ran the best organised rugby game without actually turning up. He had such a reputation as a disciplinarian that all he had to do was threaten that he just might cruise past in his car. It was enough to ensure an impeccable application of the rules and he never went near the pitch all afternoon. It was the best example of remote control refereeing I have ever seen.

There are many interesting developments in physical education. Two colleagues at Exeter University are involved in some of them. Neil Armstrong directs a health and fitness project which seems to be finding that the origins of heart disease in some people are laid down during childhood.

Even in PE lessons some children engage in little activity which drives the pulse up to the sort of rate where the heart is strengthened against future disease. One solution is greater use of small sided games where more children take an active part.

Martin Underwood is developing alternative methods of teaching which put more emphasis on children making their own choices during lessons. Martin is a brilliant teacher and watching him teach PE is to see some of the best personal and social development you will ever witness.

This kind of PE is in direct contrast to the complete crookery I witnessed in my early teaching career from one dishonest public school games master who was the most notorious cricket umpire in Britain. The uncouth state school lads I taught were invited out once a year to play the local toffs, and this villain would give you out lbw if you kicked a tin can on your way to the ground. I do not know where he is now, or if he is still alive, but if ever you pass a grave with an index finger sticking up out of the soil, he's your man.

The other day I had one of those embarrassing moments which are easier to laugh about later than at the time. We had invited two very senior people from the DES to visit us, and my colleague Richard Pring and I were invited to dinner along with them by the vice chancellor.

At the appointed time we duly assembled in the appointed place only to find it in complete darkness. Tracking down the supervisor revealed the wrong date was entered in her schedule and we were expected the following evening. The chef had gone home, and five ham sandwiches did not seem appropriate.

The vice chancellor suggested we go to a country inn which seemed a sensible idea. On arrival we discovered none of the three hosts had any money. Fortunately the restaurant believed us when we said the chap signing the bill really was a vice chancellor, but I kept cool by formulating three reserve plans: (a) the DES people could wash up, (b) disclaim all knowledge of the vice chancellor and say he was a hitch hiker we had picked up, (c) send the bill to Kenneth Baker.

A Vintage crop of prize boobs

The news that the Department of Education and Science had sold off part of a research institute which it did not actually own, completed an interesting year for Mr Bun's emporium. Perhaps it was a dummy run for local financial management, to see whether a group of hard-up governors might get away with selling off a nearby garage, or the local pub, to raise a few readies for when the bailiffs call round. It reminded me of the old stand-up comedian joke, "I've just sold my house for £5,000. The council are going mad".

It has been that sort of year. Every time someone qualified for the boob of the year award, another competitor hurled himself into the public arena and snatched away the prize. Former junior minister Bob Dunn made an early bid, when he told Parliament that the national curriculum could occupy anything from 1 per cent to 99 per cent of the school week, which clarified matters enormously. But he peaked too soon.

Optimist of the year was the primary head who replied to the consultation exercise about the programmes of study in the national curriculum by saying, "Thank you for your interesting letter about the national curriculum. We have just spent rather a lot of money on new books, so I am sorry but we shall not be introducing it".

It was nice to think that, somewhere in Britain, the flag of, albeit unintended, anarchy was flying bravely. I longed to meet the innocent who had not quite noticed all the fuss about the 1988 Education Act and thought it was optional, little realising that among Mr Bun's hundreds of newly-acquired powers was the one to rearrange the vital parts of your anatomy should you fail to conform.

Triers of the year were the many commercial firms striving to get their product into the national curriculum. I have received a variety of, in most cases, very glossily produced brochures and prospectuses, all desperate to persuade teachers to introduce such disparate commodities as flaky pastry, glass and various rubber things into the curriculum. Given a decent bit of skill at obtaining sponsorship, teachers might end up looking like world champion racing drivers, with the Whizzo washing powder logo on their elbow patches.

The unhappiest event for me was the adverse publicity about eggs late in the year. My very good friends the British Egg Information Service had made spectacular efforts to get eggs into the national curriculum and were on the verge of cracking the problem.

Eggological sciences had been assigned some 20 per cent of curriculum time, though the Big Egg himself Kenneth Baker, thought it should be 12.5 per cent and the Prime Minister wanted plenty of basic eggology. An eggological consultative group had been set up under the chairmanship of Eggwina Currie, attainment targets had been devised (at age 7 recite "Humpty Dumpty", at the age of 11 cook eggs Benedict, etc), and eggciting programmes of study had been drawn up, including cross- curricular themes like "omelettes". Take my word for it, 1989 will be the year when the yolk is right at the centre.

For those who were hoping for a quiet year after 1988, the first rude shock is the realisation that the national curriculum must be introduced in September 1989. Some secondary schools have been under the impression that they will not be involved for some time yet. This confusion has probably arisen because little has been said so far about programmes of study in fields other than maths, science, English and technology.

The rules are clear, however. All primary and secondary schools must introduce the subjects of the national curriculum in September. The detailed subject programmes must be phased in over a period of years, starting with the ones already available in 1989 and 1990. Failure to comply will mean a visit from Torquemada and the Inquisition, being given a complimentary copy of *Bun's Bumper Fun Book of English Verse,* or worse, having to buy one, read it, and then teach it as a set book.

Most important of all will be the realisation in 1989 that there is still a lot to play for. The programmes of study and attainment targets will only become repressive if people allow them to be. Good teachers have made the best of lousy exam syllabuses for years. The evidence so far is that subject working parties are coming up with sensible and, in some cases, attractive proposals that will be capable of many different interpretations.

This will be the real test for 1989. Will teaching become narrow and bureaucratic, or creative and professional? Both GCSE and the Technical and Vocational Education Initiative had the potential to become the former, but intelligent and committed teachers made sure they were much better than that. In the end the imaginative drives out the dreary. If 1988 was the Year of the Boob, then let us make 1989 the Year of Hope.

Chapter 3

Just testing

Who put the ass in assessment?

There has been a great deal of public and press concern that the new ailment which has been found in cattle could be caught by humans. The symptoms are unsteady gait and uncontrolled lassitude. A related form of the illness has now been detected in teachers.

I refer, of course, to Mad Curriculum Disease, the symptoms of which are unsteady gait and uncontrolled laughter.

I first realised I had caught Mad Curriculum Disease when I noticed people giving me strange looks as I lurched around unsteadily while laughing uproariously at my latest mailing from the School Examinations and Assessment Council. If you have not already received your *Guide to Teacher Assessment* packs A,B and C, then get hold of these three gems quickly.

They don't actually cure Mad Curriculum Disease, but they do confirm whether or not you have got it.

Take the first of the three exceedingly glossy brochures in your right hand, open it at the first page where Philip Halsey, chairman and chief executive, has his cheery "welcome aboard" statement and progress through at a steady pace, deciding at the bottom of each page whether to laugh or cry. I decided to laugh, Phil, that's why I am currently in the Mad Curriculum Disease isolation ward.

The doctors tell me that, when they first brought me in here, I was not sure whether I had been reading about measuring children or measuring curtains. The first rib-ticklers were the various checklists. Honestly, Phil, I couldn't keep a straight face. From the moment you defined the word "recently" for me, just in case its meaning had eluded me over the years, I was doubled up. The problem was that I couldn't think of any serious answers to the checklist questions. For example, in reply to the item, "Was the child puzzled, worried?" I wrote. "No, but I was".

Next, as instructed, I turned to Chapter 2 on "Test anxiety". When I read your question, "Which tasks might make it necessary for a teacher to disguise the intention to assess children?" it cracked me up again. Do you have any cute tips on actual disguises, Phil? Would it fool them if I dressed up as Santa Claus and went in saying, "Ho, ho, ho, everybody, look what Father Christmas has brought you to celebrate the middle of February, a sack full of standard assessment tasks"?

I was, by the way Phil, immensely grateful for the section headed "problems". I am glad you pointed out for me "Children do not progress at the same rate", as I would never have spotted this. Similarly, there was the helpful bit which said that "the children may 'run away' with or prematurely complete the activity". Mine just ran away with it, Phil, muttering, "Why do we have to do all this, we're only seven?" or "Bugger this for a game of soldiers", and haven't been seen since.

When I reached the section that asks whether children were frequently absent, I had to report that mine were now permanently absent, so I turned, as instructed, to Chapter 7 and the tips on how to deal with absentees. I must admit, Phil, I was a bit confused here, because your advice says, "The safest course with such children may be to increase the frequency of assessment rather than take short-cuts in curriculum delivery"

I don't want to appear churlish, but my problem is this: they're not actually here, Phil, so it is not easy to test them more frequently.

I'm afraid the Mad Curriculum Disease struck me again and I was left pounding the floor helplessly with mirth.

In any case, you know me. Would I take a short-cut delivering the curriculum? What with the one-way system round here nowadays and the van reluctant to start on these cold mornings, it's bad enough delivering the milk, let alone the curriculum.

In the same section you will recall, you ask whether "children become obsessed with your record book". Mine did, Phil, I'm afraid. Several followed me around all day trying to grab it, and one actually ate it. That solved the problem you raise under "Clipboards and checklists", when you ask if it is possible to "minimise the intrusiveness of the device."

Incidentally, Phil, I am very worried about all the reporting and recording of this caper. You know where you say "Teachers do not need reminding that planning is essential. But they may need reminding that it requires time" — well thanks again for the reminder, you're a pal. However, I did feel a teensy bit overwhelmed by all the pages of coding you suggest, such as: '10 MA 4a — understand and use language associated with angle", "16 SC 3b — be able to measure time with a sundial". The second of these is quite handy, because we can't afford a clock, but does it have to be so complicated with all these elaborate codes?

Have you any idea how long it is going to take for teachers to fill all this garbage in, Phil, even if they haven't got Mad Curriculum Disease? I gather that your outfit, SEAC, was keen to publish everything by attainment target, but that Ministers wanted something simpler. Good old Ministers, is all I can say.

We have 17 attainment targets in science, 14 in maths, between five and eight in other subjects. Eventually there will be at least 70 of these. Can you tell me, Phil, what would be the point of giving any child, let alone a seven-year-old, a string of 70 digits? And what about those who get 70 grades, all at level 1?

Do you realise that in 1992, when test scores are published, the term "level 1" will become the new form of playground abuse, replacing "thickie" and "spasmo" of yesteryear?

Finally, Phil, thanks for the mnemonic you made up to help me remember everything in your three packs, you know — INFORM, where each letter is the beginning of a telling phrase. The Mad Curriculum Disease has really got a hold on me now, so I'm not sure I've remembered it all perfectly, but I think it went like this:

> Is this monumental bullshit really necessary?
> No one who applies it to the letter will remain sane.
> For goodness' sake throw it in the bin and start again
> Only 25 hours a day will be needed
> Radically reduce the bureaucracy
> More teachers will quit the profession if you don't

It's Rasch to synergize

A few years ago Professor Stephen Wiseman pointed out that more money was being spent on research into glue than on research into education. Since then the position has become, if anything, worse. Major changes are pushed through with little or no enquiry into their implementation, impact or effectiveness. Teachers who want their classes to be glued to their seats would do better to use the real thing rather than rely on research findings.

I recently attended the American Educational Research Association conference. Australians seem to get to this monumentally important conference every year, but it was the first time for 10 years that I had saved up enough threepenny bits to be able to afford the bus fare. The story on the research front seemed to be gloomy worldwide, even in the United States.

In one symposium we were told that the American pharmaceutical industry spent nearly 20 per cent of its earnings on research and development, the Defence Department 12 per cent, but education invested less than a tenth of 1 per cent. In Britain, much effective research is being done by teachers and heads studying for further qualifications who conduct small-scale enquiries into their own school or classroom. Even that has been inhibited by cutbacks in secondment opportunities, and its part-time nature puts a lot of pressure on busy practitioners.

The pity of this is that the best research in education is very valuable. Research by two of my colleagues at Exeter University, Neil Armstrong and John Balding, showing signs of early heart disease in young children through physical inactivity and the extent of smoking and drinking, especially among adolescent girls, inform today's and tomorrow's health education programmes.

The AERA conference brings out the very best and worst of educational research. There are usually 50 or more parallel sessions to choose from and some of the lectures are excellent. At the other end of the scale is that kind of presentation that gives my finely-tuned crap-detector a nervous breakdown.

48

Ten years ago I found I needed simultaneous translation facilities to understand some of the hogwash. I remember one merchant who kept telling us how he had "synergized numerous databanks" (brought together a lot of information). This year I attended a session which should have carried a Government health warning. The topic, — recent developments in testing — should have been interesting enough, but the speaker was one of a peculiar breed of specialists in what is known as the Rasch model. I suspect they are a group of troglodytes who live deep underground, emerging once a year to bore people to death prior to a world takeover. When he stated, after a particularly brain-corroding spell "What really excites those of us interested in the Rasch model..." I got up and left, fearful whether my central nervous system would cope with the ecstasy that might follow. Don't worry, if they are Rasch enough to try to conquer the world I shall synergize their databanks.

It was notable, however, how many people did attend the sessions on testing. I found some of the American developments a complete nightmare, illustrating precisely what we must stretch every sinew to avoid. Many school districts have gone test-mad.

I visited one school where teachers had to complete every week for every child an enormous checklist of objectives which would be fulfilled in the coming week, and record the scores of the numerous multiple-choice tests which had been given that week.

The children spent so much time doing tests, and the teachers were so weary of speculating whether each pupil would be able to recognise the letter c or add two single-digit numbers by next Friday, there was little time for anything coherent. In desperation, one teacher had "vocabulary word of the day" as a major activity, which made me wonder if she began: "Good morning 3C, and today's word is "photosynthesis", so get ready to synergize your databanks".

One of the most fascinating elements of the AERA conference is the jobs mart. A huge room is laid out in the form of several booths. Teaching and research vacancies are advertised prominently, and applicants are interviewed and offered posts on the spot.

It is very tempting to apply for one of these under a false name just to see how it works. Noticing a vacancy at the University of Alaska I could hardly resist it. Slick back the hair with a bit of marge, don the glasses, adjust the smile, stride in confidently: "My name? Oh, Baker, Kenneth Wilfred Baker. Yes, I'd love to come and synergize at the University of Alaska."

When testing can become a tyranny

If there is one trend in American education we should do our utmost to avoid following in Britain, it is the headlong rush into mass testing which has taken place during the last decade in many parts of the United States.

Hundreds of schools now find themselves locked into a tyranny from which they cannot escape. American schools have often favoured regular formal assessment more than their British counterparts, but during the last 10 years it has become an obsession.

The spread of testing is based on a simple philosophy. The US, the argument goes, is a world leader in business and commerce, but often comes bottom of the league in international comparisons of educational achievements so the methods which have led to success in business must be applied to education. That means the setting of discrete objectives, regular testing of children to measure if the objectives are being achieved and the use of test scores as performance indicators, in the same way that profit levels might be regarded as evidence of success in business.

At a recent educational research conference in the US, I heard many people express their concern at the more odious effects of this test-obsessed approach to education, and was able to see at first hand its effect in the classroom.

In one school I visited, every teacher had to complete for each child an enormous checklist of 'anticipated student achievements'. This meant estimating which objectives each child would achieve out of hundreds such as 'follows three or more directions', 'identifies rhyming words', 'expresses cause and effect', 'paraphrases', 'matches colours', 'uses correct spelling', 'recombines phonemes', 'draws conclusions', 'recognises a basic sight vocabulary', these being in the field of language alone. Having made these often meaningless predictions at frequent intervals, teachers then have to test pupils to see whether or not they were right.

The multiple choice tests are organised so that they can be scored by optical scanning equipment which can recognise a shaded-in square or pencil mark, but cannot read and comment intelligently on an essay or poem.

 Observer 30.7.89

Such is the volume and frequency of testing that optical reading and scoring of test papers is the only feasible way of coping. Thus education is being evaluated not by professional judgement or pupil learning in the widest sense, but by a narrow range of easily scored and profiled tests which usually require little more than recall, recognition, or simple understanding, rather than higher order skills such as reasoning, problem solving or imagination.

The office of one principal I visited housed shelf upon shelf of blue folders containing these projections and scores, all neatly countersigned in case a member of the school board should call in. When I asked if any one ever consulted them in any detail, she confessed that they were all so shattered from completing the folders the last thing they ever did was reread them.

The consequences of this shift to test-led education are extremely serious. Innovations are judged almost entirely by their effects on test scores. Numerous teachers told me of interesting programmes jettisoned immediately if test scores fell. Yet much of what is valuable in education, be it a lifelong love of a subject, or the learning of what is really important, will not show up on narrow tests.

The proposals in the 1988 Education Act for national testing of children at the ages of seven, 11,14 and 16 will not, in themselves, produce the same stifling effect, but what goes with national testing might. If schools became so anxious about test results they they felt driven to copy American practice, then we could be in precisely the same position, especially if the press were to 'league table' schools by national test scores.

Meanwhile, American children have not moved any higher in international studies of educational achievement, and employers regularly lament the inability of a generation raised on multiple choice tests to write continuous prose.

The greatest benefits fall to share-holders in the multi-million dollar test production industry and in the manufacturers of optical scanning equipment.

Judging ability by the rule of thumb

From time to time I write something so utterly daft in these columns that I wonder whether my friends will think I have finally flipped, gone right over the top, taken leave of sanity. Then I open a newspaper a couple of weeks later and find that what I wrote is, if anything, an understatement of what has actually come to pass.

Before GCSE came out I invented a spoof 10-point marking scale for it. The bottom three points were specially for Chelsea supporters.

Grade J was given to anyone who could put a thumbprint on a sheet of paper, grade I was for those able to do a neat thumbprint, and grade H for people who could colour the thumbprint in Chelsea's colours. I now realise, incidentally, that there was a serious error here. We really needed an extra couple of lower points — grade L for Chelsea supporters who knew what a thumb was, and grade K for those who could tell their thumb from their left leg, but that is by the way.

Like many others I have been trying to sniff out what form the new national tests for 7,11,14 and 16-year-olds are likely to take. This is a most important matter because already the balance is shifting away from teacher assessments to formal sit-down tests.

We must avoid at all costs what I saw earlier this year in the United States, where many school districts have gone test-mad.

Four times each semester, teachers had to fill in predictions on enormous checklists with items like "Can blend phonemes", and then give the relevant tests. I suspect that, before long, blending phonemes could be a bigger social problem than crack. When I asked if any of the teachers ever used the test profiles, I was told that they were so knackered from filling in the wretched forms, the last thing they ever wanted to do was consult them.

Our own national tests are being field-tested at this very moment by the consortia who were given the Government testing contracts, prior to being launched on schools when the full national pilots and actual testing take place in 1991 and 1992.

I have managed to track down some items already tried out in schools. The following, I swear, has not been made up.

Some of the maths tasks for seven-year-olds go like this: first, the pupil must draw round a hand. Next, measure with cubes and then a ruler the thumb (no, it can't be) and "little finger".

How many fingers has the whole group? Guess, then calculate accurately. Use a calculator to work out how many fingers the whole class has.

Describe what a hand looks like (oh no, it's coming, I know it). Collect a thumbprint from everybody in the group (I told you, it's mad, all mad). Give a name to describe each thumbprint (stop it, I can't stand it any more).

I could not resist looking at some handprints and thumbprints that had been collected in a classroom I visited. They had been mounted and displayed on the classroom wall, but not actually given a name. It was not too difficult to think up a few, however. There was a very cross-looking one that reminded me of Miss Piggy, a bland indistinct one that bore a suspicious resemblance to the deputy head in a school I once taught in and a rather greasy one that cried out to be named Kenneth Baker.

* * *

I was sorry that Sir Anthony Meyer was treated so unkindly when he first decided to run as a leadership candidate against the Prime Minister. Some of his less sensible colleagues and certain sections of the press referred to him as the "stalking donkey" or the "pantomime horse". Nothing could have been further from the truth.

I first met him a few years ago when he was a member of the Education, Arts and Home Office Select Committee to which I was specialist adviser. We were looking at the attainments of school-leavers and I suggested that MPs should visit two schools in their own constituency. I drew up interview and observation schedules to help focus their attention.

Sir Anthony was first off the mark, completing his visits soon after I had suggested the idea. He came back full of enthusiasm for what he had seen, saying how much respect he had gained for the heads and teachers he had met and how impressed he had been at the amount of thought that had been given to what the schools were trying to achieve.

It struck me at the time how assiduously he attended all the Monday afternoon committee meetings and what a very good constituency MP he was. If only more members of the House of Commons had taken as much trouble to find out what was actually going on in schools, we might have avoided the unnecessary vilification of teachers which has been a sad feature of the fast few years.

I met several MPs like Sir Anthony who were far more impressive than some of those who actually get preferment. A number of ministers and junior ministers I have seen over the years seem to me to be nothing more than a triumph for spare-part surgery. There must be a factory somewhere that assembles them, the only giveaway being that occasionally, if you look very carefully, you can spot an ear that has been put on upside down. Then one day, they disappear, leaving only the faintest trace of a thumbprint called Wally. Have a good Christmas.

A label that will stick

Ever since I discovered that Charlie Chaplin once came third in a Charlie Chaplin look-alike competition in Monte Carlo, I have had little faith in the capacity of human beings to judge the abilities of their fellows, especially after superficial acquaintance. The proposals for testing seven-year-olds unveiled just before Christmas are chilling.

The intention is that children aged seven will be designated level 1,2 or 3 on the basis of teacher assessments and what are called standard assessment tasks. These will be administered by class teachers, but moderated externally by groups of teachers.

The difficulty of testing seven-year-olds is that they are not able to write as fluently as they can think, and many are likely to be inhibited in interview, even with a sympathetic adult.

The point is well illustrated by a conversation I had with Paul, a seven-year-old I had been teaching, when I tested his knowledge of science. Paul is, on the surface, slow and unknowledgeable. His first response, even to those who know him well, is often to say he cannot answer a question. Our conversation, about magnetism, went like this:

Ted Wragg (holding up a magnet):
Do you know what this is, Paul?
Paul (after a long pause): No
TW: Yes you do, really try Paul.
Paul (after another interminable pause): A magnet.
TW: Can you tell me what it does?
Paul (long pause, head shaking, furrowed brow): No.
TW: Go on, have a try. You often say you don't know and then you come up with a good idea.
Paul (short pause): It picks things up.
TW: That's right. Well done. What sort of things does it pick up?
Paul (long pause): Don't know.
TW: Think hard, Paul. What will this magnet pick up?
Paul (short pause): Things what's got iron in. (External moderator, if

not already on to next candidate, docks marks for poor English.)
TW (too relieved to dock marks for anything): That's right, I told you you knew a lot about magnets. Will it pick this up (holding up a piece of plastic)?
Paul: No.
TW: Why not?
Paul: Because it hasn't got no iron in it.
TW: What about this (holding up paper clip)?
Paul: Yes.
TW: Why?
Paul: Because it's got iron in it.

In the rest of the interview, Paul goes on to tell me that the magnet will not pick up a piece of brass nor a piece of aluminium (though he does not know their names), but will pick up a piece of tin can because that has iron inside it. He says that two magnets will push each other away, but when I make two stick together he says that the north end must be sticking to the south end of the other one.

It takes about 10 minutes just to elicit something from him on one "attainment target", magnetism, in one subject.

Few external moderators would have the time to win Paul's confidence or wait for his halting replies. I have no doubt that most would say he was operating at Level 1. He is, in my estimation as his teacher, performing at least at Level 2. I should be greatly irked if a more cursory view were to mark him Level 1.

No details of the moderation process are yet available, but external moderators will need to interview children like Paul if they are to make valid assessments.

If the testing of seven-year-olds is badly managed, children like Paul throughout the country will be unfairly labelled. Rather than the sensible and informal appraisal of progress which would be appropriate for seven-year-olds, national testing, as at present conceived, looks closer to the car advertising slogan — "Designed without compromise, tested without mercy".

A beginner's guide to going bonkers

I met a clinical psychologist recently who told me that she is increasingly having to deal with teachers who are suffering from stress. One of the difficulties she finds is that many people are unaware that their symptoms, ranging from rapid heart beat to profuse sweating, excessive consumption of alcohol and aggressive or bizarre behaviour, are actually caused by stress. I have set up a special task force to monitor stress in teachers. We of the Pedagogically Related Advanced Testers of Stress (PRATS) have just devised the following test to identify teachers suffering from stress.

It is raining outside and the deputy head asks you to do an extra playground duty to fill in for someone who is absent from school. Do you:

(a) Reply, "I'll just go and get my raincoat and umbrella. I would willingly do anything for you and the school".

(b) Mutter something about old Ramsbottom being away yet again so he can finish his loft conversion, and then shuffle towards the door with thoroughly bad grace.

(c) Seize him by the lapels, screaming, "You utter bastard. Have you forgotten what it's like to take 4D all morning and then have to give up your precious coffee break to stop the little perishers fornicating behind the bike sheds?"

You go down to your local surgery for a health check-up. Does your doctor say:

(a) You are in absolutely first-class health, fit as an Olympic gold medallist.

(b) I think you should ease up a bit, you're overdoing it and it's affecting your health.

(c) Either these instruments need to be sent back to the manufacturer or you are clinically dead.

You discover a sizable incentive allowance has just been given to someone less well qualified, less experienced and less competent than yourself. Do you:

(a) Congratulate the person concerned, saying, "Well done, I hope your career will go from strength to strength."

(b) Put word around that the recipient has been sleeping with the head.

(c) Storm out of the staffroom, saying, "Right, that's it. I'm off to find a job where there's a bit more sensitivity than in this place, like the local abattoir".

The chairman of the school governors comes over to you at a social event and says he is concerned at criticisms of your teaching he has heard from parents. Do you:

(a) Ask for guidance, assuring him that you are only too anxious to improve your teaching.

(b) Burst into tears.

(c) Reply, "I'll treat that observation with the contempt it deserves, since the average parent round here has the IQ of a geranium, and you yourself would have difficulty discriminating between a centipede and a duck-billed platypus".

During one of your lessons the class runs riot, breaking windows, smashing chairs and setting fire to textbooks. When confronted with this, do you reply.

(a) I am deeply ashamed of my lack of class control. Do you think I could ask the governors to send me on a course to help me improve my class management skills?

(b) Well, it's not the easiest class in the school, and I'm not the only teacher who has found them difficult over the years.

(c) What riot?

A distinguished visiting speaker comes to address the staff at an Inset day devoted to the national curriculum.
Do you

(a) Take notes eagerly during the lecture and ask questions at the end.

(b) Nod off half way through and then wake yourself up with a loud snore.

(c) Guffaw uproariously in all the wrong places, calling out at intervals, "and attainment targets to you too, squire".

How good is your attendance record? Have you:
(a) Never missed a day, even when you have been ill, because you love school so much
(b) Missed about one week per month because you find school stressful.
(c) Missed about one month per week.

A party of visiting inspectors comes to your school and one of them asks to look at your mark book. Do you say:
(a) I have devised this grid system to show the level reached by each pupil under each attainment target.
(b) I know it's slightly jumbled and scruffy, but it's more or less complete.
(c) I'm not sure whether this is my mark list or last week's pools entry, so Simkins is either at level 2 of the national curriculum or I've got him down as an away win.

When you arrive at school first thing in the morning, do you find that you have:
(a) Remembered everything and come fully prepared.
(b) Forgotten your keys and your diary.
(c) Eaten two exercise books for breakfast and packed a plateful of bacon and eggs in your briefcase.

It is two o'clock in the morning. Are you typically:
(a) Sleeping soundly so that you are fit and well for another day at school.
(b) Sleeping fitfully, waking up from time to time, wondering if you have prepared everything for your classes.
(c) Wandering round the school car park, clutching a half-empty bottle of vodka, gesticulating vaguely in the direction of the head's study and shouting. "Come out and face me you coward".

If you scored:

Mainly (a) you are probably fairly unstressed, though a bit of a greaser *Mainly (b)* you are somewhat stressed but coping

Mainly (c) You are so stressed that you are now completely round the bend. Welcome to the club. You have qualified for a free week at the Sir Keith Joseph Happy Valley Home where you will find the rest of us.

"STRESS? WHO SAYS I'M SUFFERING FROM STRESS?!?"

Chapter 4

Life at the chalkface

Escapologists with a host of skills

The news that more teachers are leaving the profession than is claimed in Government figures was disturbing. It shows, first of all, the frailty of "official" statistics. My advice, incidentally, to those seeking to reduce their school's financial deficit after a year or two of local management, is to get the Government to give an "official" estimate of the size of it. It will evaporate overnight.

A recent survey showed that 55,999,999 people feel the teacher supply situation is getting worse, and Angela Rumpty Tumpty claims that it isn't.

What is more, she told reporters, if the press refused to believe that her figures were true, then she would run all the way back up the Yellow Brick Road and complain to the Tooth Fairies in Never Never Land.

Back in the real world, however, it was also worrying to discover, from the Manchester University report which brought all this to public attention, that many teachers were leaving to set up their own business. It seemed an especially sad loss that so many people with drive and imagination are pulling out because their talents no longer appear to be valued.

All of this raised questions about the extent to which the skills acquired by teachers were transferable, especially as some commentators claimed that they were not. Yet it is equally arguable that teachers are among the most highly skilled in our society. Take something like subject knowledge. Many teachers in addition to whatever was their initial higher education in their major subjects, have acquired a deeper understanding of their field through teaching.

Newcomers to the profession often admit that they only really began to understand their main academic discipline when they had to communicate its meaning and significance to others.

I would even argue that a good postgraduate teacher-training course would benefit *all* graduates, on the grounds that it would require them to work in a community during teaching practice, turn up on time, become reliable, research their subject more thoroughly, so they could teach it effectively, and develop a wide range of inter-personal skills to enable them to relate to adults and children of different backgrounds.

Far from being unemployable wimps, teachers who have made moves into other careers have often been eagerly received by their new employers.

This is especially true of jobs where clear communication is important, and it is no surprise that a number of successful broadcasters, for example, are former teachers.

All of this set my fevered imagination racing about which aspects of teaching might be most relevant to which jobs. Oxfam and War on Want would be fruitful possibilities, on the grounds that teachers are used to working for charity. No doubt Help the Aged and Age Concern would benefit from the expertise of teachers used to wheeling their colleagues' bath chairs around in an ageing staff- room.

Those who have written school prospectuses have probably acquired the mealy-mouthed "bijou des res" language necessary to be a successful estate agent.

Teachers of the less able could manage the England football and cricket teams and those who have served on their local education committee could look after the hooligans.

Then there are the crawlers who have been soft talking senior staff to get promotion. They would have a great career in the House of Commons as a junior minister and eventually member of the Cabinet. "Licensed" teachers, being neither knowledgeable nor trained, would probably make the best politicians of all.

Autocratic heads, who operate on the assumption that most teachers are scum, could even become prime minister.

Teacher-governors could be hot air balloon champions, if they could persuade their fellow governors to speak through a long tube directly into their balloon, cruising fuel free around the world on an endless supply of matters arising and points of order. Heads could take charge of air-sea rescue, since they have unrivalled experience of being dropped in it, or finding themselves up that well-known creek without a paddle.

Teachers who have embezzled the Christmas Club funds and been put on the blacklist, the so-called Department of Education and Science List 99 (I still cannot find out what you have to do to get on to List 100), might become accountants. Some could even come back into education, under local management, as highly-paid bursars.

The trouble with teacher recruitment, supply, and retention is that it has become a major political issue.

No government would admit that it had made a complete bog-up of teacher supply. It is something which has been much more directly under political control than anything else in education, for ministers fix student teacher quotas and, recently, have determined salaries and promotion policies.

Any failings, therefore, come squarely home to roost in their own pigeon loft.

Furthermore, in the smooth post-Bun world of glossy public image, where "failure" cannot be contemplated, it is not macho to confess that there may be a crisis looming. Hence the untenable stance suggesting that there are no problems now, nor are any likely in the future. So, in this nursery-rhyme world, the 4,000 modern language vacancies created by the "language for all" policy of the national curriculum will be solved by teachers who did languages years ago, and then switched to something else, simply moving over to a modern language programme (what happens to their headship or deputy's duties, or the fate of their English or history classes is not recorded).

Nor are teachers disaffected, nor are they leaving, nor will schools fail to fill posts in the 1990s, when one in five of all the output of higher education will be needed to replace the vast number of normally and early retiring teachers.

Under fire in the classroom

"Your radio is jammed... you're pinned down by enemy fire...two of your men are badly wounded..." No, this is not a task on a management course for heads preparing to implement the national curriculum. You may recognise it as the text of a press advert for army officer recruitment designed especially to attract arts graduates.

The ad shows the above captions alongside three photographs of soldiers on the battlefield, and underneath the third of these, which depicts a man lying on a stretcher swathed in bandages, is the banner headline, "What use is a degree in medieval history?" It seems to have escaped the wizards who conceived the ad that an army officer who does indeed possess a degree in medieval history, and who finds one of his men with a wounded leg, would probably saw it off and pour a bottle of whisky over it.

All of this set me thinking along two lines. The first was that this could be the style of the new Department of Education and Science recruiting literature for El Cheapo licensed teachers. There could be photographs of children sitting on the chest of some hapless untrained licensed teacher, hiding the chalk, pinning him against the wall or throwing paper aeroplanes at him, and the text could read: "Your mind is blank...two children are sitting on your chest...your classroom is on fire...", followed by the banner headline, "What use is your diploma in basket-weaving now, smarty pants?"

The second strand of thought was a much more serious one about the notion of "relevance" in education. The answer given by the copywriter of the army officer ad to his own question about the utility of a degree in medieval history reads: "A lot of use. You have a trained mind. The capacity to absorb information rapidly and to act on it. It could save the lives of your men. That is why we value graduates of any discipline." In other words, the assumption is that skills acquired in one domain are transferable to another.

This raises several issues about the purpose and style of education, whether in the context of the Technical and Vocational Education Initiative or the national curriculum. It is interesting that major employers, like the armed forces, are going out of their way to hire people who appear, on the surface, to have had little "relevant" preparation.

There are aspects of human learning where it does make sense to learn in sequence a set of "relevant" skills and then combine them into an organic whole. Certain sports require very specific skills like passing or running with the ball, and practising these singly and together is "relevant" training. On the other hand, in a game like snooker there is no real point in practising separately the art of walking round the table, even though snooker involves a lot of it, because anyone not actually on a life support machine can do it already.

We learned to walk because we were motivated to do so, and we learned it in a form which is generally useful by walking whenever it made sense or there was a need. If someone had tried to put one of our feet in front of the other at an early age as a detached part of a self-conscious, "relevant" structured skills package, we would probably have nose-dived more often than we did.

This highlights one worry I have about the implementation of the national curriculum, especially in primary schools. Some people seem to be under the impression, because guidelines and attainment targets are expressed as discrete pieces of behaviour, that these are topics which must be taught in sequence and ticked when completed.

This rigid notion of teaching, which is, thank goodness, being discouraged by the National Curriculum Council, would go against what we know about how young children learn. Sometimes they do learn directly by tackling a topic or skill head on, but equally often they learn in a more oblique way.

Most of us have learned to smile not because we successfully completed a single "relevant" course on smiling but rather as a result of several inter-related experiences. The challenge to teachers is to judge, for each requirement of the national curriculum, whether it makes sense to cover it separately, or organically, or both.

Enough of the boring stuff. Let me finish by telling you about a Puffin book for young children I have just read, entitled, I tease you not, *Master Bun the Baker's Boy*. It tells of master Bun who is browned off with his present job and desperately wants to be a butcher's boy (Home Secretary?), dreams about being a bank robber's boy (Chancellor of the Exchequer?), and finally becomes a conjuror's boy (Prime Minister?). I loved it, especially when Mr Creep's dog ran off with his sausages.

IT'S QUITE A CHALLENGE MAKING FRACTIONAL DISTILLATION MORE INTERESTING THAN SEX

Enthusiasm will certainly help. You can recognise teachers who have spent at least five years in the profession, because they actually do find fractional distillation more interesting than sex. Those with more than 10 years can no longer tell the difference between fractional distillation and sex.

A good sense of humour will not go amiss, either. Especially when you see your salary cheques. Not only will it help you to keep the attention of a class, it will also help you deal with the difficult bank managers you will certainly encounter at some time or other.

Equally important, though, is a strong imagination. Especially when you think of what you could be earning in other professions. For it is on your creative abilities that you as a teacher must continually draw, just as I have had to dredge desperately the depths of mine to find anything positive to write in this awful copy.

Of course, there are topics that have to be taught at the blackboard. Getting on for a couple of thousand of them at the last count, and a few more national curriculum documents still to come. But in every subject there is still tremendous scope to express yourself in unconventional ways.

Since all 2,000 topics are legally required as well, you can always express yourself in unconventional ways by throwing slates off Strangeways roof when they lock you up for failing to deliver.

Visits, discussions, debates, films, fieldwork and projects are all methods teachers use to make learning much more fun and their lessons more effective. Discussions and debates are best because they are also cheapest. Under local management, of course, visits, films, fieldwork and projects will take second place to mending the roof and paying the pittance you will receive from the governors for your labours, so they are out for a start.

Incidentally things like films are not, strictly speaking, "methods" at all, and in any case videos are more common nowadays, but I'm only an agency copywriter who's been told to make all this sound like a ring-a-ding picnic, so let's not be pedantic. I'll not bore you with all the rows you'll have about which parents pay and which don't if you are ever foolish enough to arrange a visit. You can find more about that in the fine print of the 1988 Education Act, which is a damn sight less interesting, it should be said than either fractional distillation or sex.

Although more interesting lessons involve more work, (they've asked me to say that, just in case the fun approach appeared a touch overdone), you'll have the support of your colleagues to help you. Those not too bewildered, knackered or already in the funny farm, that is.

Any teacher will tell you how rewarding (though not in cash terms) it is to be able to spark off (that reminds me, arson can be a bit of a problem in some schools, mainly staff incinerating national curriculum documents) an interest in your subject (all right, so nobody told me that primary teachers have to cover the lot. I'm only a copywriter, so get off my back will you? Well, it pays the mortgage, which is more than you'll be able to do).

If you are interested in a career in teaching and would like more information, ring 0334 300121 quoting Department code UTTER/CON or fill in the coupon below. If you have the right qualities, we can certainly provide the challenge. Send for our booklet SUCKERED INTO IT today.

I have swallowed this garbage, hook, line and sinker, so please rush me your booklet SUCKERED INTO IT.

Name _____

Birth _____

Address _____

_____

_____

Postcode _____

I am (tick as appopriate) a graduate ☐ mad as a hatter ☐ suggestible someone whose shoe size and IQ are identical game for a laugh ☐ a fully paid-up masochist ☐ extremely rich, so who cares about the salary ☐ more interested in fractional distillation than sex ☐ wondering who agreed to spend £2,200,000 on these adverts.

It's yes, yes, yes, with the DES.

Stop the world I want to get off

A Few years ago there was a popular show running in the West End entitled *Stop the World, I Want to Get off.* There is a sporting chance that a revival would be packed out with 400,000 teachers and heads looking for a way of stopping the spinning carousel of reform and counter-reform on which they currently find themselves. In the coming year they will be implementing the National Curriculum, coming to grips with local management, taking part in compulsory teacher appraisal which followed the 1986 Education Act, and no doubt encountering other novelties as the year progresses.

This raises a host of questions about the nature and purpose of change, like how much, why, when and with what priorities? Too little change leads to an unhealthy inertia, but too much causes a series of stressful conditions well catalogued by Alvin Toffler in his book *Future Shock,* such as overload of decisions and ad hoc solutions to problems. The pressure on heads of schools in particular was aptly summarised by one primary school head replying to a series of questions asked of 900 primary teachers as part of the Leverhulme Primary Project we are conducting at Exeter University. He described his most recent week like this:

"This week I have had a range of in-service: Wednesday a day on appraisal: Thursday a day on local management of schools; Friday a day on proficiency and assessment and Friday evening to Sunday afternoon a weekend course on the role of the new governing bodies. When do I find time to give my and my staff's attention to the National Curriculum? We are shattered! Everything is being introduced at such a rate we cannot reflect and get to the heart of the matter".

All change

When I sat down with my co-author John Partington to write the book *Schools and Parents* and also to rewrite our 1980 *Handbook for School Governors* we discovered the list of topics we needed to introduce was enormous. There were four major Education Acts in the 1980s, those of 1980, 1981, 1986 and 1988, which had given parents and governors more powers, changed the organisation of schools and local authorities and introduced our first ever national curriculum.

In addition there had been the GCSE reforms and other new examinations such as the Certificate of Pre-Vocational Education and the A/S Level, the introduction of more technical and pre-vocational education and the advent of profiling and numerous other 1980s buzzwords. We had to include two chapters on parents' newly acquired rights and responsibilities in *Schools and Parents*. In the case of *Handbook for School Governors* half the book was thrown away at the start and completely rewritten because it had become hopelessly out of date and the rest needed quite a major overhaul.

Faced with a lot of changes people tend to react in various ways, some of them largely defensive. Over the years I have seen teachers who could cope with the greatest of upheavals without breaking their stride and those who were reduced to jelly if the start of their 9.15 class was changed to 9.20. One head I knew was a bit like a mountaineer. Each change was like a new peak to be climbed and you half expected to meet her in the corridor armed with rope and ice-pick, off to implement GCSE or introduce new style school reports. In contrast, I can recall a head and deputy known to staff as Weary Willy and Tired Tim after the two erstwhile comic heroes for whom the arrival of the morning post was a body blow.

Resistance

One of the more stylish ways of resisting change is to pretend you are not only in favour of what is being proposed, but that you have actually been doing it for years. This allows you to carry on delivering the same old rubbish whilst appearing to be a pioneer at the very cutting edge of reform. Another master strategy is to say that you are waiting for the novelty to be properly evaluated before taking the plunge and giving up your tried and tested methods. Everyone knows that evaluation of reform in Britain is about as common as polar bears in the Sahara, so that ruse is likely to see the perpetrator safely through to retirement.

It would be easy to practice the best known defence to change, that known as 'Denial' whereby you simply pretend that nothing is happening and hope it will all go away. Unfortunately it never solves any problems. The most successful heads and governing bodies will be those that can establish sensible priorities and then implement them. It is not humanly possible for schools to make all the changes required of them in the short time scale allowed, but judicious selection of the highest priorities at least helps steer it in a positive direction.

Why teachers want to quit

The recent Gallup poll findings that over a third of teachers are thinking of leaving the profession and well over 90 per cent feel undervalued came as no surprise. Anyone in close touch with schools for the last five or six years has been well aware of the serious decline in morale.

It is not explained solely by the speed of change. Many primary schools changed dramatically in the 1950s and 1960s, producing excitement rather than bitterness. Teachers accept change as the inevitable precursor of improvement. But when they are at a low ebb, rapid change becomes one more source of aggravation, especially as, since the 1988 Education Act, they feel excluded from planning the nature and direction of reform.

Nor is it solely explained by salary levels. Although teachers, like other groups, want to be paid adequately, if money were all that concerned them many would have pursued an alternative career. Most teachers were recruited in the 1960s and early 1970s when pay was not princely. Only briefly, in the mid-1970s after the Houghton Award, were they a little more affluent. In classical times Lucian equated teachers with kipper sellers in terms of poverty, and sometimes in recent years teachers would have been glad to be that well off.

The main reason for present disaffection can be explained by a combination of one major factor and several minor ones. The single greatest blow to teachers' morale is dealt by the low public esteem in which they are held. It is not so much at the individual level, because parents and members of the public, if asked, say they feel teachers are valuable members of society.

The biggest influence on self-esteem comes from politicians, especially ministers, and from the Press. The process began with Sir Keith (now Lord) Joseph when he was Education Secretary. Increasingly, suggestions of teacher incompetence figured in his speeches, which were then widely reported. Like any profession teaching does contain a few duds who are an embarrassment to their hard-working colleagues. No one felt the topic should be sacrosanct, but Joseph's constant harping on about incompetence and his reluctance to praise began to grate.

70

Then, in an election campaign, Mrs Thatcher described education as "disaster area" — a theme quickly taken up by newspaper articles and readers' letters beginning: "It is now recognised that schools have completely failed the nation", as if that were to be taken for granted. Yet in its own 1985 paper, *Better Schools,* the Government said: "There is much to admire in our schools; many of them cope well, and some very well, with their increasingly exacting task," going on to quote with approval improvements in curriculum and examination success. But this received less publicity than its demands for reform.

The arrival of the media-sophisticated Kenneth Baker in 1986 made things worse. While Lord Joseph, brow permanently furrowed, uncertainty etched on every feature, gave the impression that he was probably not in touch with the schools, Baker's apparent certainty was much more wounding when he attacked teachers. Particularly hurtful was an interview with *The Times* in February 1988 in which he said he had been angered by the "600 reasons" which teachers had found to oppose the Technical and Vocational Education Initiative — when, in fact, it was teachers who had made it work.

It has been noticeable in the recruitment of young teachers how many have commented that friends already in the profession had tried to put them off. This is so different from the past, when teachers seemed to enjoy their job to the extent that many of their pupils wanted to seek the same satisfaction. Now most tell pupils that, given their time over again, they would have done something different.

In the face of so much adverse publicity, relatively poor pay and other factors also weigh teachers down. They had their negotiating rights taken away when Kenneth Baker dismantled the Burnham Committee on the grounds that it rarely agreed about anything. If ability to agree were the sole criterion of the survival of a democratic institution, the House of Commons would have been shut long ago.

The long periods of industrial action of two and three years ago were undertaken reluctantly, and as a last resort. I know of whole staff rooms where everyone voted to strike, often with not a revolutionary among them. The woman deputy head of an infants' school once told me in tears: "If people like me vote to strike, what has it come to?"

It will take some years, and a wiser, kinder breed of minister, to win back the good will. It is too late now, I am afraid, for Kenneth Baker to offer belated praise in his speeches. The damage has been done.

It will need a much more genuine recognition of the worth to society of good teachers to attract newcomers in sufficient numbers and to raise the spirit of the profession. Three out of five are over 40 and in no mood for further disparagement.

Management by pure hokum

There are six words which, when uttered in the right tone of voice, can strike terror into the very marrow. Grown men quiver; seasoned professionals shake at the knees; holders of the Victoria Cross hide under the nearest large sofa. If you want to empty the room fast, just say to your colleagues: "I've been on a management course".

Now don't get me wrong. When Sir Keith "Come-back-all-is- forgiven" Joseph announced a few years ago that he was going to spend a million trillion pounds on improving school management, I was all in favour. I was a bit bemused when I heard that he had originally wanted to give it all to British Oxygen to train school heads, because I could not quite see what trundling cylinders of oxygen around the world had to do with nurturing the nation's youth, but perhaps it was meant to revive fading staff who needed a quick sniff of the stuff.

Anyway, as far as I was concerned management courses were things you gave to other people. Only the barmy or witless actually went on one. After all, one had one's amateur status to think about. Now I have to confess that I have actually succumbed and been on one myself. Not one of those interminable jobbies — I'm not totally daft. Just a few days spread over the year with the odd residential spot to cement the Dunkirk spirit.

I have been fascinated by these courses since the 1970s when the "in-tray" exercise was popular. This consisted of unlikely memos from people like the caretaker complaining about untidiness in the art room. I have never met a caretaker who actually writes memos. Most have a rather more direct form of communication. But it was fun.

When asked to put in a guest appearance at a management course, I have usually talked about the curriculum, relationships, improving classroom skills and teacher morale, or helping children learn something, in the simple belief that these were the most important aspects of management and the rest was pure hokum. I have always refused to purvey any of the passing fads on the grounds that I could not do it without bursting into hysterical laughter at the sheer limitlessness of human gullibility.

Notions like "management by objectives" have always creased me up. In the clean textbook version, managers write down long lists of objectives and then faithfully implement them. As an optimist I have always believed in the intelligence of action. Work out something sensible and then do it. When you look at it afterwards the implicit objectives always seem a lot more intelligent than the banal explicit objectives that get written down in a "management by objectives" exercise.

Management courses are notorious for being run by someone who could only organise a game of ludo with several assistants, but this one was well-run. There were the obligatory John Cleese films. All the stuff about dispatching sprockets to Darlington is about as relevant to an educational establishment as life on Pluto, but it was decent comic relief.

We had the usual group exercises which in theory helped us to be members of a team. One involved sorting out two jumbled up jigsaw puzzles. I ruined it by spotting that one of them had a thin dark streak in the ply, so our group broke the world record. The organiser was a bit upset because we should have fallen out, chosen leaders and that sort of thing. I thought that management was sometimes about finding a short cut rather than herniating yourself.

Then there was the mandatory session on "stress management". Most of us were completely laid-back before it started, but the fellow who gave the lecture was taut and hunted — wound up like an anxious whippet. By the end, we were all bloodshot nervous wrecks.

I watched on television a piece about a management course for industrialists. It seemed a great consolation that these apparently shrewd entrepreneurs were willing to part with thousands of geeenbacks for the pleasure of being led blindfold through a swamp, in the unlikely hope that it was character building. My 13-year-old son would have done it for a fiver.

In the final session we had to write down anything which had influenced our practice. My brain went into auto pilot, but I did recall setting up two in-trays after the session on time management — one for urgent, the other for less crucial matters. The only problem was that I tended to share the mail democratically between the two of them, wanting neither tray to be upset. The air was blue last week when both of them fell on my foot, so I am about to launch the latest, all-the-rage fad. It will be called "management by invectives".

Teacher trouble

The teaching profession is currently caught in a fork. The right prong represents the view that it is a demanding profession requiring considerable skill so teachers must be selected artfully and trained rigorously. To ensure quality control a special accreditation machinery, the Council for the Accreditation of Teacher Education (CATE), was established to vet teacher training courses.

The left prong represents the view that almost anyone can teach without too much ado. The best manifestation of this belief came in the government Green Paper on qualified teacher status which was published earlier this year.

It proposed that anyone with any post A-level qualification should be given the status of "licensed teacher" and allowed to teach immediately in a school for a probationary two- year period. After that the person concerned would be a qualified teacher.

The right prong represents the late 20th century professional notion of teaching, the left a 19th century sub-professional apprenticeship model. The contrast is stark. No government would dream of asking any other profession to resurrect its 19th century practices.

In the 19th century Dr Andrew Bell and Joseph Lancaster developed a monitorial system which was eventually so heavily criticised it was scrapped. Newcomers were put straight into schools after, Bell boasted, 24 hours of training. Lancaster first gave them a series of lectures on "the passions".

Today new trainees have to meet strict criteria. CATE lays down that they must possess relevant A-levels or degrees, complete a course usually lasting four years, study a major subject at degree level for at least two full years and undertake significant periods of supervised teaching practice.

The same government ambivalence applies to experienced teachers. On the one hand they are told that teaching is an extremely arduous profession and many of them are not up to it; on the other hand, the Government has virtually killed opportunities for secondment for teachers, reducing full-time university places from over 2,000 to 600 in a single year, and allowed precisely two days for teachers to be trained to teach the new GCSE examination.

So why is the Government moving the teaching profession back into the 19th century? We recruit some 11,000 new teachers a year, about one in 12 of all the people in higher education. By the mid-1990s we shall need more like 20,000 a year, and with a falling population of 18 to 21 year olds that could mean one in five of all students in higher education.

The Government faces the acute embarrassment, therefore, of not having anticipated this problem until it is far too late. The alternatives available are limited: much larger classes, scrapping the new National Curriculum because it cannot be staffed, dragging anyone before a class who is not actually on a life support machine, or bursting into tears.

It is easy to predict how this lowering professional standards option will be launched. It will begin in the new year when the Government issues a consultative paper on the training and recruitment of teachers. The first line of attack will be to drive a wedge between teachers and teacher trainers by saying that teacher training is too theoretical, that all training could be done in about 1,000 schools as the responsibility of governors under the new local management set up by the Education Act.

Yet the recent HMI report on teacher training in universities recognised the substantial changes which have taken place in the last few years and commented on the generally good partnership between training institutions and wide variety of schools.

Flooding the nation's schools with untrained "licensed teachers" might pass unnoticed by the general public for a year or two, as would a similar dismemberment of medical training, but the outcry later would be enormous. It is the wrong time to return the teaching profession to the last century.

Last words from the rip-off factory

Dear Parent,

Quite a lot has been happening in the school since newsletter 21, so I am writing to bring you up to date. I am delighted to say this will be my last ever parents' newsletter, as I am quitting as head at the end of this term. When I looked at the early retirement deal, I realised that, for doing nothing at all, I would be earning nearly as much as I get now for herniating myself every day.

Indeed, if I took the current school crossing patrol vacancy, I could make up much of the difference by standing outside the school, morning and evening, holding a big lollipop stick. For all the good heads can do nowadays I might as well spend all day standing *inside* the school holding a big lollipop stick. So this will be the last of my mealy-mouthed biennial missives, in which I try to paper over the remorselessly spreading cracks.

The biggest change since my last newsletter is the introduction of what is grandly known as local management. This is a joyous misnomer for a system whereby I have to manage the Government's curriculum and the Government's testing programme with a sum of money determined by the Government's formula. In other words it is about as local as the Katmandu Wimpy Bar.

The result of this latest wheeze to give power to the people has been worked out by a formula whose subtlety, I must admit, eludes me. In so far as I can actually understand it, the local authority has to think of a number, add to it the IQ of the chairman of the education committee, (which in our case, I suspect, may reduce the sum), multiply it by some civil servant's hat size and then take away the number you first thought of.

As a result we are some 30,000 smackers worse off and must sharply reduce our expenditure. I have been asked to tell you of the manifold and hare-brained schemes dreamed up by the governors to meet the shortfall. Great hope has been invested in the entrepreneurial powers of your own offspring. If we do live in an area awash with such a rich pool of wealth generating genes, then I am left asking myself why the whole neighbourhood looks like the set from a World War Two film, but that is by the way.

The governors have been convinced by the chairman, whose own chip shop hovers permanently on the brink of oblivion, that we can ape those schools whose pupils are said to be making millions on the side, so we have joined the mini-enterprise scheme. For those whose dustbins are not yet full of child-manufactured junk, let me explain what joining the mini-enterprise scheme will mean in our case.

Your children will in future spend valuable school time manufacturing a succession of substandard, hideously mispainted garden gnomes. Under the mistaken assumption that this will put Britain back on its feet, (and having seen the junk shortly to be launched on an unsuspecting world, I would advise Britain to remain lying peacefully on its back), you will then be expected to feign delight at this manifest garbage, and, no doubt through clenched teeth, actually part with your hard-earned loot to purchase it.

The staff meanwhile are supposed to believe that this rip-off teaches children the meaning of market forces and prepares them for a glittering career in the big world of business, and I suppose to some extent it does. Thus not only will the school make a fortune, it is being argued, but your children will all become millionaires. I have pointed out that, for the second part of this prediction to come true, the great British public would have to consist of millions of people with the critical acumen of an educationally subnormal midge, but my words are ignored.

You may have read about those schools which are levying a £50 voluntary charge on parents to pay a teacher's salary. Our governors are proposing a Rent-a-Teacher scheme instead. For a tenner one of my colleagues will come round to your place and clear a blocked drain, paper over a crack or make a silk purse out of a sow's ear, in other words more or less what they spend the day doing anyway. As you can imagine the National Union of Teachers is delirious about this.

If you wish to take advantage of this scheme, I would advise you to avoid Mr Fosdyke, unless you want the same chaos in your home as we have daily in the school. The pinnacle of his efficiency is to remember to give out the pencils, and successful completion of his attendance register is hailed as a major administrative triumph, the staff holding a dinner to celebrate.

I am afraid that my own brilliant fund-raising suggestions were dismissed by the governors as the demented ramblings of a demob-happy loon. Thus the coin-op toilet scheme ("10p a pee" was my rather snappy slogan) was not adopted, which is a pity, as we could have had the unique distinction of being the first school in Britain to erase its LMS debt by widdling it away; a fine example to others, I would have thought.

Nor was my suggestion to set up chatlines any more successful. Given that parents have complained for years that they can never discover how their children are getting on, it must be well worth 38p a minute to phone up and find out. Mrs Hardacre, whose classroom voice has always reminded me of the speaking clock, (the content of her lessons has the same level of intellectual power, it should be said), could have told you the time, as her eyes are on the clock most of the day anyway.

Fortunately I have managed to raise a quick hundred myself. I discovered that a local firm was willing to pay £50 a skip for waste paper, so I soon dispatched a couple of skips. It is too early to say yet how the Chief Adviser will react, when he visits us next Tuesday, to the 12 empty shelves in my study which used to house the school's collection of national curriculum documents, but I will let you know. Suffice it to say that the postman who delivered them all gleefully helped me load up the skips, and I have promised to buy him a new truss out of school funds.

My successor was asked one question at interview, namely, "What are you like at raising funds?" Personally I would have installed a cash dispenser in the vestibule and saved the salary, but I am proud to be able to hand over the gnome factory in tiptop condition, as I sign off accordingly.

King Gnome

" WE'D BETTER LET THE CHIEF EXECUTIVE DECIDE ..."

Chapter 5

LMS — Lots More Suffering

The Chief Executive

Once upon a time, long ago, there was a person in charge of each school who was known, promise not to laugh, as the headmaster, headmistress, head-teacher, or simply the head. Now look, Level Nine, I've warned you before, if you want a national curriculum grade 15 for this study, you can jolly well listen to what I'm telling you. Jenkins, stop behaving like a Level 2 will you and just keystroke the title, if nothing else. It's "One hundred years of Private Education, 1988-2088". All right? If you don't pay attention I'll ask the chief executive to reschedule you for home study.

Now, where was I? Ah yes, following the 1988 Education Act, which is generally regarded as the starting date for universal private education, the role of these so-called heads — Jenkins, what is it now? Look girl, have you not accessed the central database to find out what the 1988 Education Act was? I did ask everyone to modem the 1980s video in advance, so that you would all know what this session was about.

Lights on if you have already watched the second segment of the 1980s video, the one that deals with social issues. Well, that's not too bad, 95 per cent of you, but I do expect Level Nine students to be mature enough to modem videos when asked. Yes, Peterson, the smooth looking man with the flat hairstyle and glasses is indeed the same Baker that fundraising Baker Days were named after, and no, I do not know why he was always smiling, as he disappeared into obscurity in 1992 when he left politics and bought a second- hand car business.

Now for goodness' sake let's get back to the topic or you'll all be national curriculum grade 14 for another semester. As I was saying, in the early 1990s all those people who had previously run schools under the title of headteacher were replaced by what we nowadays call chief executives. I suppose, in retrospect, it was rather foolish to expect someone who had never run a business to be in charge of a school, but, odd as it may seem to you today, 100 years ago it was assumed that a person who had been a successful teacher could actually take responsibility for a school.

Anyway, it soon became clear that ex-teachers were not going to adapt to running a business. A few did actually try. Some raised a paltry 10 or 15 per cent of the money needed to run their school in the transition period towards privatization — pathetic by modern standards. However, it was really the school bankruptcy scandals of the early 1990s and the School Bankruptcy Act of 1998 which introduced five-year jail sentences for chief executives of schools that had run out of funds, that eventually sounded the death knell for old-style headteachers.

To be fair, the Government of the day did try. Prime Minister Heseltine personally saw through Parliament a series of Bills which were meant to help chief executives who had been teachers. There was the 1993 Filofax Act which granted every ex-head a free personal organiser, the 1994 Electronic Mail act which gave them their own computer, word processor, modem and personalised fax number, and the 1995 Charities Act which allowed them to go busking in school time, but all to no avail.

By the time the legendary Reg Ratface, or "Rob 'em Reg" as he was known in the popular newspapers, had been dismissed in 2003 for standing at the school gate with a sawn-off shotgun, demanding money each day from students before they had even entered the school yard, the writing was on the wall, as they used to say when schools were covered in graffiti. It was a mere formality by 2005, when the notorious Solihull Six were sacked for holding a discussion on the curriculum contrary to the 2001 National Curriculum Act, that the last few ex-heads would all be fired, as indeed they were.

What I'd like you to do before next Thatcherday's lesson is... Jenkins, right, that's it. I will not have students reading a book in my classes. You're fined 5,000 Euromarks. Take your credit card to the chief executive immediately and ask him to reschedule you for home study in future. After all, that is what he's here for.

Local authorities

Right, listen Level Nine. I've told you before, if you want a national curriculum grade 15 for this module on "One Hundred Years of Private Education, 1988-2088" you're going to have to pay attention, otherwise I'll get the chief executive to reschedule you for home study. Then you can find out for yourself just how easy it is to get off grade 14 with only your video-modem to help you.

Now today we'll be looking at the role of local authorities prior to the full privatization of education in 2008. What do you mean, you don't know what local authorities are, Fotheringay? Did you not access the late 20th and early 21st century social structures video, like I asked you to? I sometimes wonder why I bother. If teacher strikes weren't a capital offence I'd withdraw my labour some days, I can tell you.

Well, for the benefit of Fotheringay and anyone else whose work station was on the blink last night, let me recap events for you. Back in 1988 the country was divided up into 104 administrative zones so far as education was concerned. Each of these was called a local education authority, or LEA for short.

When, in the early 1990s, schools were given their first push into privatization by taking responsibility, at local level, for finances, hiring and firing of teachers and various other matters which are taken for granted nowadays, some LEAs began to dissolve. It started simply enough with the dismissal of staff after the 1995 Charities Act, which offered a bounty of a new building and up to a half a million pounds in cash, that's about five million Euromarks in today's currency, to any school opting out of its local authority. This bounty system had already been operating informally since about 1990, but making it official immediately encouraged half the schools in the country to leave local authority control.

The outcome of all this was that the LEAs were left with very few staff and their only function was to support a small number of schools, mainly in poorer areas. As their revenue from the Government decreased, their problem increased. In the end it seemed kindest simply to abolish them, and this is what happened some years later when Education Minister, Sir Oliver Letwin, took his 2008 Education Privatization Act through the House of Thatcher, which had replaced Parliament two years earlier.

Even though this Act was originally known as "Olly's Folly" there was little resistance to it because education was, by then, the only unprivatized service. Some LEAs tried desperately to put on a few courses for teachers and chief executives to ensure survival, but most preferred to attend courses at newly privatized polyversities and teachers' centres, so that particular hope for survival soon dried up.

Now what I'd like you to do before next Thatcherday's lesson is to write a comparison between last year's 2088 Education Act and what we've just been talking about. The exact title is "Give a historical critique of the more controversial aspects of the 2088 Education Deprivatization Act", so let's just discuss it before you leave. Any suggestions?

Yes, Peterson, I think it would be fair to say that the present Government feels nostalgia for the 20th century and has made the issue of Elizabethan values a central plank of its reform programme. Indeed, you may find that its plans to group clusters of private schools together under 100 regional councils to improve efficiency, and then finance them with Government-provided and locally-raised money, has some similarities with what we have just been talking about.

Quite right, Sanders, it should be more effective to offer services to schools from a regional centre instead of each school providing its own at high unit cost. And yes, we shall have to wait and see, but you may also be right in guessing that each school will, in future, no longer need to employ its own part-time educational psychologist, its 10 professional fundraisers its 11 part-time national curriculum advisers, its four senior and six junior accountants and its two lawyers.

What's that, Fotheringay? While we're at it we could what? Put all the schools in London together, yes, go on boy, it looks promising, and set up a new single regional authority for the whole city, yes, go on, this sounds brilliant, and call it, what did you say? Go on boy, speak up, the Inner London what?

Information

There was once a school where the staff found that many of the letters they were giving to pupils to take home to their parents were not being delivered. Everyone was deeply worried about all this vital information not reaching parents because the children forgot to hand over the important little brown envelope when they got home. The head decided to take action, so he wrote a letter to all parents saying how worrying it was that some children were not delivering messages properly, put copies of it into several hundred little brown envelopes — and gave them to the children to take home to their parents.

You cannot help sympathising with the poor beggar. How to communicate with one's fellow humans has been a problem since the dawn of time. I suspect that there were probably Twelve Commandments originally and either Moses forgot one of his tablets of stone, or whoever was responsible for making the record nodded off at the moment Moses read out the last couple. Number 11 was probably "Thou shalt not assume that anyone is listening to a single word thou art saying", and number 12 may have read "Thou shalt not believe that the invention of telephones, word processors and electronic mail will make all that much difference to thy communication problems".

Transmitting information efficiently is a difficulty at all levels. Communication between the head, who is often the first recipient of letters and bulletins, and the rest of the staff, or between staff themselves, given that everyone is very busy, is often a problem. At the next tier, there are breakdowns in communication within the local authority and between it and its schools, and at national level the same can be said about communication within Government departments and between the national and local arms of government.

Solutions begin with the entirely traditional, like finding the biggest gossip in the place and telling him or her that what you are about to reveal is a tight-lipped secret. At the other end of the scale are sophisticated modern systems, usually based on the micro-computer.

It would be entirely wrong to assume that modern electronic systems completely replace oral methods. However inefficient the use of the human voice may be, it still has a part to play. The effect of the printed word is cold by comparison, and though this may not matter in many circumstances, it can count for a great deal in others.

Take memos. I always find it irritating when I receive a long typewritten memo containing matter which could just as easily have been uttered on the phone, or face to face. The best use of a memo is when the written word is needed for clarity or for the record.

In larger organisations the use of electronic systems will one day have a place. At present I would have to say that electronic information storage, retrieval and conveyance remain a source of some frustration. Take the storage of data about new curriculum developments, for example. It is not, on the surface at any rate, a bad idea to log into a database details of who is doing what in various schools.

Unfortunately there are serious problems. The first is that most systems are quite good at planting but not so clever at weeding. It is infuriating to ring up someone whose project you have picked up from the database and find that it has now been discarded or the person concerned has left. Much of the information on databases is throwaway, but is not being thrown away.

The second is that most systems are undiscriminating. Some of the databases I use for research have a massive collection of so- called "research". In practice both the one-page bright idea while shaving and the three-volume five year mega-project are logged in together, given their set of descriptors and their 300 word summary as if they are all equivalent. Quality control is desperately needed.

There is no doubt that both the simple and the complex have their place in modern communication. Whereas we could do with more of the former, we often get more of the latter. I think people working in education will simply have to be patient with the electronic modes until they become more refined. Ten years ago, few journalists or businessmen would have been able to tell a fax machine from a fandango. Now they are commonplace. As one of my colleagues keeps telling me, the only way he can tell his fax number and his telephone number from his salary is that the salary has far fewer digits.

Staffing

My father used to dream of having £1,000. He never made it, alas, but in his youth it would have been five to 10 years' wages. Today it would pay for about three weeks of supply teaching, mend a modest stretch of roof, hire a part-time secretary for a few hours a week, term-time only, buy a ton of reasonable apples, 5,000 Wispa bars or 400 bottles of Piesporter Michelsberg from a supermarket. Best to buy the bottles of plonk, then you won't care about other possibilities and priorities.

That teaching and non-teaching staff should be seen in cash terms against other possible expenditure money is a relative novelty. Until now, though it was known that staff costs accounted for well over half the local authority's budget for education, this was not a matter for individual schools to worry about. In future the bill for staffing, and hence the effective use of human resources, will be a major concern, and this will bring gains as well as losses.

The first, and in some cases most spectacular effect of transferring staffing costs to schools, is the creation of winners and losers. Local authorities have been doing numerous computer runs, based on recent figures, to see what schools are likely to get when their historical funding gives way to formula funding. The result of these dummy runs has usually been complete mayhem. Losers, typically well established schools with mainly top-of-the-scale teachers, can "lose" tens of thousands of pounds. Winners, sometimes new schools with younger staff, can "gain" similar amounts. The adjustment will be painful for many.

The positive side of this will be to make governors and senior staff in schools think very carefully about the deployment of teaching and non-teaching staff. The negative side is that many schools, particularly the bigger losers, will have to decide between hiring a teacher and an ancillary, or even whether to make some staff redundant.

There is no doubt that the climate will change within the school community. The employer-employee relationship is subtly different from that which exists now. If a teacher's wrath, rightly or wrongly, is directed at

County Hall, a Dunkirk spirit can develop in the school, even among those not involved.

Among the staffing problems more likely to be dealt with by governors in future, (indeed some of these are in evidence already), are the following: the replacing of a teacher by one in a different subject; the non-replacement of someone who has left; the replacement of a teacher with a licensed teacher or ancillary; the refusal of secondment on salary; the non-replacement of absent teachers by supply teachers; and staff redundancies or redeployments. Heads and governors well used to diverting anger about these issues to the local authority will find it painful to be on the receiving end of the steel toecaps.

On the other hand, there may be interesting changes in the management approaches which find success in the new climate. Any governing body which tries to be too macho with staff will soon see the ugly effects of this style of management. With professional people the better way forward is to make sure they are involved in decision making. There is much less hostility when a group has had to conclude that an unpopular decision must be taken, than when one is imposed on them.

Over the next few years, finding out how teachers can be used to cover the national curriculum will be a major challenge. There will be a strong temptation to advertise for someone who can teach maths, science, technology and English, but who is willing, when necessary, to help out with geography, history, art and music, take a teeny bit of PE and, should the need arise, speak fluent Spanish and Russian to help with the modern languages diversification programme. Since Tarzan is not likely to be available (in any case he is strong on practice, but weak on pedagogy), it will be as well to involve teachers themselves, thus harnessing collective brain-power to these mind-bending strategic decisions.

Marketing

Last November the Government brought out a new set of requirements for all initial teacher training courses. There was an enormous list of topics and activities to be covered, but, unless I missed it, nothing about running raffles, busking, carving you own begging bowl, fleecing parents, sawing off the end of a shotgun, or any of the other ruses heads and teachers might have to get up to in future to raise revenue for the school.

Nor is there anything about image making, or marketing the school, which is probably just as well because many trainees have a wicked sense of humour, as well as a lively imagination, and might send the whole thing up. Yet the common complaint, particularly of people in senior positions, when faced with such demands, is "We never trained for this sort of thing".

It is quite true. Initial training establishments are not the Harvard Business School. If they were, then new recruits to teaching would be especially nifty at marketing and fundraising, but useless at teaching, because they would have done their teaching practice on Madison Avenue. The question arises, therefor, whether schools should train up certain key people, like the head and deputies, to become marketing experts, or, since any pretence at expertise might be a sham, whether they should simply hire specialist individuals or firms to do the necessary.

Perhaps I have been unlucky, but the fundraisers I have met have been characterised by one serious disability, namely the inability to raise funds. It is a bit of a handicap. I can think of two who managed little beyond their own fee, and I would counsel anyone thinking of hiring someone who talks a good game and spouts on about "the American experience" to be extremely wary. "Never mind the American experience, sunshine, how much have you actually raised in your time?" is the key question.

Such tactics as chasing former pupils, establishing a list of firms willing to fund projects, persuading parents and other friends of the school to covenant money, are all quite fruitful in certain areas, but less promising where there is not a great deal of spare wealth. Also, a school needs to investigate carefully what it will get in return for any fees it pays to an agent.

There is no point in paying a large retainer to someone who will merely write a few letters or make the odd phone call. If you lay out real cash, make sure the recipient will be running his socks off, thus saving the staff time to get on with the job for which they were trained.

At the selling stage, fundraisers will sometimes talk in telephone numbers and make hopelessly optimistic estimates of what they will achieve, but then they are hardly likely to underestimate. Keep a large bag of salt handy when listening to them. The same applies to external marketing experts who try to sell schools new images, and logos. At the going rate of £30,000 to £50,000 for a new logo, which is often just a capital letter or something less attractive than the school badge, only the foolish will be separated from their cash without a struggle.

There is no doubt that many schools could have presented themselves more effectively in the past. The answer, in my view, is not to hire some expensive image maker, but rather to capitalise on what the school already has. For example, there is usually at least one enthusiastic, credible and articulate member of the staff who would be good with local media. It may be the head, but equally it may not, and the heads should not feel they have lost face if they ask a member of staff to act as friend of the media.

The art of presenting the school in a good light is first of all to identify its good points. These need not be spectacular, because little of what features in local media is. Next, think of a newsworthy angle, because this is what broadcasting and print journalist have to do in order to persuade editors to give them space or air time. When 14,000 schools took part in the BBC Domesday Project, for example, many managed to get favourable local press coverage. Although the "Pupils survey Britain" headline was newsworthy in its own right, after a bit this lost its appeal to editors. But "Swinesville School pupils identify need for a sports and leisure centre" did not.

Remember that journalists are usually busy and welcome a story in a form in which they can use it without too much editing. A well- written press release can be invaluable. Write it so that it can be used in various forms, like the first paragraph only, or the whole thing. Keep it down to one page of A4 if possible. Give it an eyecatching, but not over-the-top headline. Name a contact person and give a telephone number so anyone wanting more information can ring up.

Finally, get to know local journalists and find out their deadlines. No one will give space to a story which arrives a few minutes before a deadline. Get all this right and you will inform parents and the community about the good things you do, gain a well-earned favourable image for the school, and save a fortune in marketing consultant fees.

Performance indicators

When discussion moves to the topic of performance indicators I must declare a small handicap which gets in the way of rational analysis. I can't stand them. Whereas other people are able to move into their "on the one hand, on the other hand" mode, it is one issue on which I cannot be ambidextrous.

The whole idea, as recently conceived and advocated, seems knuckle-headed to me, an illustration of the dominance of the accountancy ethic, a passing fad which will be ridiculed for its crudity in the 21st century. The word "performance" is alien to much of what education should be about, and many of the criteria that have been posited do not indicate "performance" so much as describe conditions, many of which are out of the control of teachers, though they may well be blamed for them.

Take two commonly-advocated performance indicators, social background and examination grades. If school A has more children from professional and socially privileged backgrounds than school B, is this purely an indicator of performance? Should the teachers in school B have somehow hijacked, cajoled and kidnapped more socially well- endowed children through their doors, and is it an "indicator" of their failure that they have not done so, or is it merely that they are located in a clapped out, down-town area frequented by the less affluent? If Smoothville grammar school pupils obtain better GCSE grades than Scrufftown secondary modern, is this an "indicator" of better teaching or merely confirmation of the selection policies of five years earlier?

Supporters of performance indicators would say that this is not the way to use them. Social class, they would point out, is not in the same category as exam scores. It is an indicator of initial differences and should therefore be used as a basis for the "value added" approach. In other words, you should discount the effects of social class before considering examination grades, so that you really measure what the school has added to pupils since entry.

I could just about go along with this notion were it feasible. There is, unfortunately, no agreement about how to compensate for initial differences. It is not like a handicap race in horseracing, where you simply load the better horses with agreed extra weighting, based on past form, so that the race finish is closer. If Liverpool Football Club beat the Scruffville Cubs XI by 23 goals to nil, would this be a good result for them or for the Cubs? What ought to be the handicap? If it is 10 goals to nil then Liverpool did well. But they are a professional side, so maybe they should have triumphed by 150 goals to nil, in which case it is a phenomenal performance by the Cubs.

When such statistical techniques as multiple regression and analysis of covariance have been used to modify the effects of initial differences, it has always been controversial. If this is done to the league tables of exam scores in local authorities, many of the South- east LEAs move nearer the bottom of the table and the northern cities move towards the top. No one is really convinced by it all.

This leads to another problem, that well-recognised medical phenomenon *league tableitis* or the urge to display any quantitative information in the form of a league table.

Estate agents and local newspapers are the main sufferers, but even the national press is not immune.

Last year, when the Universities Funding Council produced its annual volumes of totally indigestible performance indicators, *The Times* ran a story with a huge graphic containing league tables, saying that Cambridge University was best at getting students through exams. In my own subject, education, Cambridge had a 100 per cent success rating, as did five other universities. All nine students who switched into the education tripos at Cambridge did indeed complete. So did all six students at Swansea. Aberdeen University must have been over the moon about their one student managing to graduate, albeit after six years. Just imagine if the poor beggar had failed — zero per cent, bottom of the league, relegated to the GM Vauxhall Conference League, and Aberdeen sick as a parrot.

At the end of last year, Angela Rumbold launched a more muted version of the performance indicator scam, saying a school should choose "a relatively small range of indicators for judging whether it is achieving its goals". Government guidelines, none the less, list a set of 50 criteria grouped under five headings, staff and pupils, social background, pupils' attitudes and achievement, parental involvement and management issues.

At least there is no national scheme and with luck, therefore, league tableitis, like smallpox, may one day be eliminated as a major health hazard. I have absolutely nothing against compiling a checklist of important issues which schools can use to take stock of what they do, with the involvement of outsiders if an objective view is sought. Indeed, many schools which have practised self-evaluation in an intelligent way have taken this as their starting point.

It is the crass and uncritical use of purely quantitative information to make meaningless comparisons which is odious. That approach should now be buried in a lead container 1,000 feet underground on Easter Island.

New Liberties Made Simple

For those who are still confused about local management of schools, even after the past six weeks of pull-out supplements in *The TES,* here is the final definitive version of all the essential terms and concepts.

Q   I am still unsure what LMS actually stand for. One of my colleagues insists it is a now defunct railway company, but other tell me it has something to do with schools. Can you clear it up once and for all?

A   Linguistics experts are divided about the origin of the term. One head thought it meant Let's Move South, so he retired to the Costa del Sol. Current opinion favours one of three explanations: Lend Me Sixpence, Lots More Suffering and Left Me Speechless.

Q   I do not really understand how teachers' salaries work nowadays, though I think they are fixed by a body call the IAC. Is it true that governors will be responsible for handing out bonus payments for teachers under LMS, and can you explain the rather complicated set of what I think are called Insensitive Allowances?

A   You are quite right. Since the abolition of the Burnham Committee the Government has set up a body to determine teachers' salaries, known as the IAC, which stands for It's A Carve-up. There are five extra allowanced for teachers which governors can distribute for different purposes. Allowance A is for Apathy when you can't think what else to do. B stands for Bribery, because it is often used to keep good young teachers who threaten to move elsewhere. C is for Come on Sunshine, as this is the reply from teachers who feel they are worth a great deal more. Allowance D stands for Desperate, because it is frequently the only way of recruiting or retaining someone in the shortage area, and E equals Every Blue Moon. There are rumours that the Government may extend the scheme with three additional grades — F for Forget it, G for Greasers and H for Ha Bloody Ha.

Q   The LMS supplement which dealt with salaries for senior staff like heads and deputies said that, from January 1991, there will be 49 points on the senior staff salary scales, and that a head or deputy can move up at the discretion of the local authority or governing body in the light of national criteria covering responsibilities, the school's catchment area and his or her performance. How will this work?

A   There was in fact misprint in this particular supplement. Instead of 49 points, it should have read 49 *pints*. The criteria determine how many pints the head or deputy should be given. Those who are already walking somewhat unsteadily should only be given one pint, or even no more than a half of lager shandy. People working in a difficult area can have 48 or 49 pints.

Q   The head of our school is insisting that LMS requires massive changes in everyone's titles and duties. He has put to the governors a proposal that he should be renamed Absolute Supreme and Unchallenged Chief Executive and Ruler of the Universe and be given a pay rise of several thousand pounds. At the same time he is proposing to devolve most of his duties to myself, his deputy. Now he has ordered me to rename my job. I cannot think of a suitable title. If I am no longer to be called deputy head, can you suggest a good name for me in the future?

A   Sucker

Q   I am not entirely clear where to find out about teachers' conditions of service. The LMS supplements mentioned something about a Burgundy book for teachers and various kinds of books covering other people who work in the school. Can you clarify this?

A   It is all quite straightforward. Teachers' conditions of service are published in what is known as the Burgundy book, because Burgundy is what you will need a bottle or two of, if you are ever foolish enough to try to read it. The secretaries' version is published in the Tasteful Lilac, Scented With Just A Hint of Miss Dior book. The conditions of service for PE teachers can be found in the Faded Loughborough Purple book and those for CDT teachers in the book with the leather patches on the spine. The deputy heads' version is published in the Extremely Sensible Black Shoes book. Caretakers' conditions of service are available in the Dark Brown With a Few Oily Stains book, which usually can't be found but is thought to be down in the boiler-room or somewhere about the site.

Q   I have lost the very useful checklist from the LMS supplement on the maintenance of premises. Can you just remind me what it said?

A   What is the state of the roof? (a) sound (b) in need of repair (c) no longer there. What are the walls like? (a) recently decorated (b) peeling (c) covered in rather primitive looking paintings of mammoths and sabre-toothed tigers. Who is responsible for the maintenance of your church school? (a) the vicar (b) the diocesan body (c) God knows. If you had £250 to spend on school repairs at the end of the financial year what would you do? (a) mend holes in the drive (b) buy a snooker table for the staffroom (c) put it all on a horse and gold plate the school if it came up.

Q   Our local MP recently addressed a conference of school governors and told us that LMS will give us a lot more freedom. Can you spell out what this will actually be?

A   Certainly. You will have freedom to go bankrupt if you overspend. You are free to devote all your spare time to raising extra money. You will be at liberty to spend six hours at governors' meetings trying to make ends meet. You also have complete freedom to have a nervous break-down at any time of your own choosing.

Q   I cannot remember the details now, but there was some mention in one of the supplements of a special group of individuals who may act as LEA trouble-shooters once LMS is in place. What do you call those people who will deal with schools' difficulties, bail the school out when there are cash-flow problems, rescue the governors if they are in danger of losing face, smooth things over with parents, and take the blame when things go wrong?

A   Teachers.

Chapter 6

A governors' guide to...

...*Chairs*

Being asked to chair a governors' meeting is probably not unlike stepping up from the back-benches to become a Minister, apart from the absence of a chauffeur-driven limousine, your own private detective, a large salary, an army of civil servants and a huge carpeted office. In fact, come to think of it, it is probably nothing like becoming a minister, so any delusions of grandeur should be shed from the beginning.

The job does, however, carry with it quite a deal of responsibility, only some of which is related to running the meetings. Given that governors meet once or twice a term, in usual circumstances, there is all the time in between, often as much as four months, when important decisions have to be made. On matters like staffing, pupil discipline or relationships with the local authority, the chair may have to speak or act on behalf of the whole governing body. It is not a job for the faint-hearted.

Chairing meetings effectively is an art in itself, as anyone who has witnessed it being done well or badly can testify. Good chairs know how to get a meeting out of a quagmire by saying, "Let's see if I can sum up our discussion so far", and then making the issues seem much clearer, so that reaching a sensible decision becomes more likely.

They also pace meetings effectively, and are not afraid to hustle people along, aware that if the governors spend too long quibbling about petty matters on piddling item three, they will not have enough time for important agenda items six and eight.

Bad chairing can completely ruin any chances the governors have of being an effective group. Being an incompetent chair is also quite an art, and some stereotypes are, alas, alive and well. There is the *soloist* who likes the sound of his own voice so much he does not permit others to interrupt any of his arias. The *expert* is another pain, since he feels duty-bound to pontificate on every conceivable matter, even on buildings, just because he once built himself a back porch, which probably fell down.

Then there is the *little me,* a clever, disarming one this, because he protests that he of course, knows nothing about such matters, and then goes on to reel off the past 30 years of the Department of Education and Science statistics which he has been learning by heart in the library all night.

Watch out also for *Genghis,* the autocrat who tries to force his own views on the board as if they are the consensus of the meeting. I was once present at a committee chaired by a Genghis who took a vote thus: "Those in favour please raise a hand". All 19 hands went in the air. "Well I'm against it", he rejoined and went on to the next item.

Preparation for meetings is most important. The only thing worse than members not having read their papers in advance is when the chair has not read them either. It is easy to recognise these chairs because they usually say: "Now this item is very important so I'll just read out to you the relevant parts of the paper". The halting delivery and occasional surprised tone in the voice is a dead giveaway.

So, if you are asked to chair a governing body try to be fair and honest, not sly and scheming, listen, don't just talk, be tender as well as tough, and support the governors and staff rather than dominate them. If anyone ever tells you that you are "chair material" just remember that, although chairs can be made of silver and gold, many are made of such materials as wood, plastic or foam rubber. And everyone agrees that the worst chairs usually needs stuffing.

Heads

If ever you go to a conference about education and want to know, out of all the teachers, administrators, governors, journalists and politicians, how to recognise the heads who are present, nothing could be easier. Just look for the people picking up litter. It is symbolic both of the proprietorial role and the uncomfortable fact that if you want anything doing you might as well do it yourself.

The quickest way to commit suicide nowadays is not to hurl oneself off a high building but to stand up at a meeting of heads and shout out "early retirement". As you are trampled to death, the last words you will hear are "Where?" and "I'm first".

Not to put too fine a point on it, heads have had a bellyfull during the past 10 years. They kept schools going during the worst period of industrial action anyone can remember, and many did lunchtime supervision on their own for months or even years. Just in case any were feeling bored, they were faced at the same time with falling pupil numbers, all the problems that contraction brought, a shortage of cash for books and equipment, and a torrent of government and local authority directives.

Yet despite these formidable problems, the many good heads in the system managed to keep up the morale of their staff, respond to most, if not all the demands on them, and establish or maintain good relationships with parents and governors. Far from castigating heads, as some newspapers and politicians did, we should have been urging captains of industry to visit well managed schools and pick up a few tips, just as heads have been willing to learn from the best practices in industry and commerce.

There have been considerable changes in the styles of headship over the last decade or two. The autocrats who ruled purely through the exercise of coercive power, whose sole concession to the modern notion of "consultation" was to read out a list of their decisions at the beginning of each term, may not have disappeared completely, but they have given way to much more open breed of head (and by that I do not mean one who knifes you in the *front*).

Michael Rutter's study of effectiveness in London secondary schools found that, in the relatively successful ones, teachers were more likely to feel involved in decision making. Alienation is not just something that happens to young people on the fringes of society. It can also be experienced by teachers and it is a potent factor in schools with a poor head.

Now that governors have a much more important presence in education, good heads make sure that they too feel part of the team, and avoid giving the impression that all lay people are idiots, even if some are. Only the inept boast to their friends or colleagues about having their governing body stitched up, failing to realise that it is probably untrue, and even if it is accurate, someone will almost certainly grass on them.

It is because the best heads are so good that the poorer ones stand out. Some, alas, have simply buckled under the pressures of the last few years. Others are what is known in the trade as "pre- retired", which means they have died on the job and been allowed to stay on posthumously.

The introduction of compulsory teacher appraisal also applies to heads, and it is no surprise that the cost estimates of appraising a head are usually some six to eight times those for appraising a teacher. My own view is that, although a few duds should get a low rating, most heads, and indeed their very professional deputies, who have also become an important part of the educational landscape in the past few years, deserve 5.9 for both technical merit and artistic impression.

Villains

So far as discipline in school is concerned, never believe what you read in the papers (apart from this one that is). People whose daily reading is confined to those newspapers which choose to sensationalise education are convinced that schools are riddled with violence and that, by contrast with the classrooms and corridors of their local school, New York subways must be a haven of peace and tranquillity.

Nothing could be further from the truth. When Her Majesty's Inspectors conducted large-scale primary and secondary school surveys, they concluded that nine out of 10 primary teachers could obtain absolute silence whenever they wanted it, and that only six and a half per cent of secondary schools had serious discipline problems. On the whole, the same nutcases who tear up the terraces of their local football club on Saturday afternoons are fairly well contained in school from Monday to Friday.

When I did an analysis of hundreds of lessons as part of the Department of Education and Science funded Teacher Education Project, I found that only one per cent of the parts of lessons we analysed contained misbehaviour more serious than noisy chatter, which was the most common "offence". What is unconvincing about film or television portrayals of classes rioting is that the director has told everyone to misbehave. In the frisky classrooms of real life many pupils would do nothing more than look bored and wait for something interesting to happen.

The "villains" in real classrooms, therefore, are not razor- wielding thugs with a cauliflower ear and a nice line in extortion (and that's just the teacher), but rather show-offs, gossips and wits whose sense of humour is not always shared by others.

There is a sinister minority of violent pupils who represent a real threat to the community, and governors should certainly become involved if any of these attack a fellow pupil or a teacher. Physical assaults on teachers can undermine the whole community and must always be dealt with in a manner which restores confidence rather than compounds the problem. The suspension (nowadays called "exclusion") of a pupil is something which must be used sparingly, but it is difficult to see how it can be avoided in serious cases of assault on teacher or pupil.

Classroom troublemakers are not very different from what they used to be. Generations of pupils, especially adolescents, have perfected that facial expression known as "dumb insolence". It is notoriously difficult to punish. Pupils can protest that they have actually done nothing wrong and that the face they were given is in any case down to their genes, so why not stick their parents in detention?

In primary schools especially, "fidgeting" is another source of bother, with causes ranging from bright pupils who are under-employed to acute haemorrhoids. Thus the treatment of what appears on the surface to be the same problem must vary according to the cause. Setting a page of quadratic equations may end the boredom of the intelligent pupil, but is not normally recommended by doctors as a cure for piles, though that may well change if there are any more national health service cuts.

Most difficult are often the pupils who distract and incite others, and appear to be confident and macho about their role as classroom disrupters. I once lost patience with a big 15-year-old boy who had caused bother to all his teachers throughout the year, and told him to stay behind at the end of the lesson so that I could sort him out once and for all.

When the bell sounded he waved a brassy goodbye to his departing mates and I waited apprehensively for the classroom to empty. As the door closed behind the last one to leave, to my utter surprise he burst into tears. There is no single explanation or treatment for those who cause trouble in school, and this apparent big shot was in reality as self-confident as a jelly baby.

Teachers

In classical times, Lucian equated teachers with sellers of kippers. In terms of their financial rewards, there have been times recently when many would have been glad to be that well off, and the loss of good teachers, especially those in their twenties with a maths or science background, has been a sad feature of the mid Eighties.

The last 30 years have seen a crazy roller coaster pattern of teacher recruitment. In the early Fifties there were 200,000 teachers in England and Wales. As both Labour and Conservative governments strove to bring down class sizes and the large cohorts of baby boomers moved through the educational system, this total went up to 300,000 by the mid-Sixties, 400,000 in the early Seventies, and 479,000 by 1980. Today we are back to nearer 410,000.

The consequence of this up and down graph is that three out of every five teachers in primary and secondary schools will be over 40 by 1990. The denim-clad trendies of the Sixties will have turned into a host of Phyllosan-swiggers in the Nineties. This has both advantages and disadvantages. The biggest plus has been the wealth of professional experience now available in most staffrooms. The new GCSE exam, introduced under much less than ideal conditions, would have been a complete flop if it had been launched in similar style in the Sixties when staffrooms were full of inexperienced rookies. It was accumulated expertise which rescued it. The minus will come if middle-aged teachers refuse or find it hard to change their teaching strategies in future and become inflexible.

One of the most important responsibilities of governors comes when they find themselves on a selection committee. Armed with their "papers" those magical and mystifying trappings of bureaucracy, which in this case encapsulate the career and aspirations of the four or five poor beggars who will parade before them, they must pick their winner.

"Now viewers, you at home can join in. Press button A if you think they should choose the beginner with an upper second BA in Serbo-Croat and a primary postgraduate certificate; button B for the former secondary teacher with a BEd in metalwork and Sumo wrestling and five years' recent experience in a primary school; or button C for the old lag who trained 30 years ago, but has a winning smile, a warm personality and is magic with slow learners". (No contest, pick the old lag).

One problem faced by parent governors is the professed anxiety of many about being on a selection committee at all. This is based on the mistaken assumption that they have been put there as Britain's leading expert on curriculum development, when in truth they are there as parents saying how they would feel about each candidate teaching children like their own.

It is true that some lay people ask idiotic questions that have teachers keeling over with mirth in the pub afterwards. A politically nominated chair of governors is reputed to have welcomed a candidate who had a doctorate, and thus the letters DPhil after his name, with a cheery "Come in, Phil". Whether he called all the rest "Ed" is not recorded.

The worst sin, by lay or professional person, is when interviewers allow long-standing prejudices to prevent them looking at the person rather than the stereotype. That way good teachers who have worked in ILEA, taught in a grammar school, grown a beard, supported Leeds United or bought a pink lipstick, waste their journey for no good reason.

Some questions are barely worth asking. I await eagerly the first candidate honest enough, in reply to question "Do you like children?", to answer, "Personally I can't stand the little perishers, but it's a living, squire". In the right company that could be worth a headship.

Fashion

There is one way never to be out of date so far as curriculum fashions are concerned, and that is simply to wait long enough for your favourite idea to come round again. It is the same with clothes. The very same early Seventies flares, which had my son clutching his sides with mirth when I was foolish enough to wear them a couple of years ago, will be the height of modishness this winter, mark my words.

That is how the 1904 regulations, with technology replacing what used to be woodwork for boys and needlework for girls, became effectively the first version of the national curriculum set up by the 1988 Education Act. If you want to see what the school curriculum might look like in the year 2000, you could do worse than interview grandad about his schooldays.

What does change is the detailed content, and, increasingly of late, the teaching styles to go with it. The best recent example of that is the reformed GCSE examination, which certainly features maths, science, history, geography and other subjects familiar to generations of pupils, but not in the exact form in which they knew it.

Music was radically reconceived to weave together listening, composing and performing. Many pupils used modern synthesisers and wrote and performed brilliantly original works. In modern language courses the excessive practice in translation to and from the foreign language, which used to dominate lessons in the Fifties and early Sixties was replaced by an emphasis on using and understanding both the written and spoken word in everyday situations like shopping, travel and family life.

The enormous explosion of knowledge, which prevents even the cleverest of human beings from knowing more than a tiny fraction of what has been discovered, has produced three pressures on the school curriculum. The first is the need for *selection* of what is taught. We cannot know everything, but we must know something, so someone has to draw up a syllabus, hence the arguments about what the various subjects of the national curriculum should actually contain for children of different ages: when in a health education programme one should cover drug and solvent abuse or dental care, or whether pupils should study the Saxons at seven, nine, eleven, or at several stages.

Since we can know only a fraction of what it is possible to study, the second pressure is for children to acquire the *processes* of lifelong learning, the ability to find out for themselves, to know when to read rapidly or slow down and take notes, to use modern technology like the micro computer and the interactive videodisc, all vital, since most will have to retrain more than once in their adult lives.

Third, it is important for children to work in *groups,* because many problems in future will not be solved by individuals but by teams. It is true that no committee would ever have composed Mozart's symphonies, but no individual could make and launch a space satellite.

Not that these fundamental principles necessarily determine all matters to do with curriculum fashion, which can be as ephemeral as clothing or pop music fads. English teachers would probably die nowadays rather than set an essay title like "A day in the life of a penny", "A ride on the 69 bus" or any of the other favourites of yesteryear.

Will teachers in the year 2010 crack up at today's favoured ideas such as "investigation" in mathematics, "empathy" in history (mind you, that's a bit of a giggle already), or "experience-led learning" in technical and vocational education? And whatever happened to Old Lob, the beloved old horse of my childhood reader? Probably enjoying a well-earned pint down at the knacker's yard of curriculum history, alongside the original Beacon Readers, Whitmarsh French, School Certificate chemistry and Durrell maths, all waiting patiently to be recalled for curriculum service in the year 2025.

Tests

The story is told of the person sitting at a desk filling in a personality test. One question asks, "are you decisive?" He fiddles with his pen, chews his fingernails, hesitates and half starts to write several times, furrows his brow, and finally, after several minutes of anguish, writes "Yes".

That illustrates one problem with tests of many kinds, namely the great difficulty of measuring behaviour or performance accurately through pencil and paper assessments. If you wanted to know someone's skill at tightrope walking, it would be better to ask them to demonstrate their art rather than write an essay about it.

Yet all kinds of judgement are made about children, and indeed adults, on the basis of what they are capable of writing down for an hour or two in a crowded room on a hot sticky day in May or June. Our desire to hang labels round people's necks for easy reading seems insatiable. Thus it is easier to process the knowledge that someone obtained grade B, or was given 62 per cent, than to listen to a much more long- winded tale about their helpfulness, ability to work harmoniously as a member of a team, or some other vital aspect of personality or performance.

As a result of our voracious appetite for testing, a whole examination and assessment industry has been built up, with its own language and conventions. There has been a shift away from the traditional type of exam, known in the trade as "norm-referenced", where you simply spread the candidates from about 20 per cent to 80 per cent, with 50 per cent as an average mark and most people scoring between 40 and 60.

Not that variations to that time-honoured format are unknown. We are all familiar with "criterion-referenced" assessment through the driving test, though no one actually throws away his L plates and tells all his friends he has just passed a criterion-referenced test. People have been locked up for less.

In order to become a qualified driver we have to meet *all* of a set of criteria. There would be no point in saying to the examiner after your driving test, "Look, I know I mowed down that policeman on the zebra crossing and then reversed into his squad car, but I must have scored 80 per cent on the rest of the test, so surely that is good enough for a pass mark overall". On that sort of test you either meet the criteria or you don't.

This is closely related to another great issue in assessment, the need for more *diagnostic* testing. If you are a primary teacher, being told that a pupil scored 12 out of 20 in a maths test, or obtained a B for reading, is of limited value. Much better would be to receive a profile showing what mathematical operations, say using fractions or understanding decimals, a child can or cannot handle, or learn what sort of words and phrases a pupil finds difficulty with when reading.

For me, however, the greatest issue in assessment is not the wholly laudable development of a wider range of techniques, such as profiling and diagnostic testing, nor the emergence of new styles of examination like the GCSE and the Certificate of Prevocational Education, which is taken by pupils at 17 and based entirely on profiles. It is rather the excessive prominence given to labelling.

When one puts a "third class" label around the neck of a bottle of wine, it does nothing to the wine itself, whatever effect it might have on the producer. Do the same to seven-year- old children and many will accept the label as a permanent judgement of their ability. The nation is full of adults who believe they are thick because of what happened at school. Many are quite wrong and have unnecessarily limited their lives and aspirations. We cannot afford to depress future generations in the same insensitive way.

Budgets

When I was a student I had a friend who was money-mad. Every time the conversation took a turn towards cash, his eyes would light up with luminous £ signs. At the time Peter Sellers played a similar character in the *Goon Show,* and whenever he saw an opportunity to make money there was the sound effect of a cash register in the background. We all used to imitate the cash register bell when talking to our friend, and he became known as "ding". He is probably a school governor by now, chairman even.

As financial management is increasingly undertaken at local level, governors who have never previously had responsibility for much more than the odd couple of tenners permitted them by their spouse, may find themselves faced with a budget running from a quarter of a million, in the case of a modest sized primary school, up to a million pounds plus for a secondary or community school. Sales of hand-held calculators will soar.

The world of the accountant is not quite the same as that inhabited by the rest of us. There is much talk nowadays of such notions as *cost benefit analysis* or *performance indicators.* Some of these principles are genuinely helpful ways of getting the best value for money. Others are nothing more than the usual mystique within which all professions shroud themselves in order to preserve their power or impress the gullible.

Cost benefit analysis is quite a useful technique which might easily be applied to a real life situation. Suppose, for example, your school acquires 50 extra pupils and the appropriate cash to go with them, but you are short of accommodation. A cost benefit analysis would work out the true cost of say, four different options: (1) to build a new two-classroom unit, (2) to lease a temporary portable building and place it in the school yard, (3) to renovate an older decrepit building, (4) to rent a couple of classrooms from the church next door.

Since most of us would not have the faintest clue, off the top of our heads, which of these four options represents the wisest investment of money, a cost benefit analysis is very helpful. It might show, for example, that the new building, which looks dearest on the surface, is cheaper in the long run because of lower maintenance and fuel costs, or that the leased building is cheaper because the extra intake is a one-off and will be through the school before long.

What it will not tell you about is the *qualitative* side, which of the options you feel would be most conducive to good teaching and effective learning. That is where governors' intelligence comes in. Similarly, performance indicators, which compare one school with another in terms of teachers' salaries, books per pupil, exam results and so on, have a limited value and must be monitored by human insight.

Your school may be dearer than another not because of financial incompetence, but simply because the teachers are older and on a higher point on the salary scales. There are various hilarious mickey takes of accountants' performance-indicator reviews, commenting, for example that the double bass player in the orchestra did not seem as busy as the others, and was he, therefore, really necessary?

So another whole new vocabulary awaits school governors: the land of *virement* (being able to shunt money from one heading to another, eg "books" to "equipment"), *consortium buying* (getting together with others to obtain bigger discounts) and *insolvency* (honest, M'Lud, when the bailiffs came I had no idea. I thought the figures in our budgets were in red because the head had bought a new typewriter ribbon from the consortium at 30 per cent discount). All the best with it. Ding, ding.

Consumers

The words "consumer" and "consumerism" do not flow easily off the tongue in education. For a start there is some doubt about who these consumers are. Often one thinks of parents, but employers who take on the products of education, pupils themselves, the direct recipients of it, and indeed all of us in any society, are entitled to claim that we must have a say and some rights.

The second problem with the word is that the notion of "consumption" always suggests that resources are going down the drain at a rapid rate. Fair enough if one is talking about the only true consumption in education, school dinners, but not right for a meagrely endowed school, carefully husbanding its limited supplies.

The whole push towards greater accountability in education has certainly given more prominence to the views of the public at large during the last few years. The needs of employers are constantly stressed, though they are often seen as a narrow minded lot looking for factory fodder, when in reality most are simply asking for children to leave school endowed with basic skills, willing to learn and able to show up on time. It is parents, however, who have been mentioned most frequently.

All the magazine articles about parenthood show a proud mother nestling a newly born baby, with a beaming father in the background. The whole is surrounded by yards of lace and soft toys. If they showed instead pictures of parents after sleepless nights, the mopping-up-mess ritual, primary children who have difficulty learning to read, teenagers for whom raising an eyebrow represents the limit of any physical exertion that day, or families mugging the postman on GCSE or A level results day, the human race would be extinct inside a couple of generations.

The 1980s has seen a rapid rise in the number of rights for parents, such as the right of appeal if their choice of school is not met, access to statements written by professionals if their child is mentally or physically handicapped, or the right to be full members of school governing bodies. Nevertheless we still have an ambivalent attitude towards parents. There are essentially, in our minds, two major types. There is the group in the white hats, to which we and our friends belong, who are good eggs who support their children, are the salt of the earth, and never put a foot wrong.

The other group, in the black hats, to which the rest of humanity belong in our simple scheme of things, comprises feckless, uncaring, no-good layabouts, who spend most of their lives in the pub or watching television and do not give a fig for education. There are indeed parents who do not come to school functions because they have small infants or elderly relatives to look after, or those who are a bit prickly when they come to see a teacher or the head, because they are apprehensive or not very skilled at raising delicate matters with a professional person, but none of these belongs to the black hat brigade.

Even the white hats have some funny cards. As a teacher I always used to try and guess, before parents' evening, what it would be about parents that explained their children's behaviour. I was often wrong. I was once dying to meet what I imagined to be the long-suffering, careworn, meek mother whose son was always in trouble for never listening to a word I or anyone else said. When she strode across the room and turned her laser-like voice on me, uninterruptably vaporising every eardrum in sight, I realised her son was in fact a genius who had learned that the only way to survive the blast was to go psychologically deaf.

Perhaps we should concentrate far more of our attention on the pupils themselves, the real consumers. Although some forms of education — much of what goes on in the primary school and several secondary developments, such as the Technical and Vocational Education Initiative — have tried to put children's views and needs centre-stage, they are still often left out.

Yet thousands of hours are spent by politicians, professionals, adults generally, and governing bodies in particular, speculating about their needs. I wonder how many governors have spoken to a representative sample of pupils during the last year. Why have meetings been arranged, publicity produced and rights drawn up for everyone except the people who matter most, the pupils?

There is nothing to stop school governors having a joint meeting with them to discuss the future of the school. There would need to be a simple agenda, and children might be apprehensive at their first meeting. Let them produce some written statements beforehand, and appoint spokespeople to speak on particular matters, and let governors develop the skills of listening and encouraging without overawing. It would be an important piece of self-development for all concerned. Put away this newspaper and go and arrange it this very minute.

Chapter 7

Politics, Politics

A challenge for champion losers

The concept which lies at the very centre of the Government's thinking, if that is not too ambitious a word, on education, is that of "competition". The assumption is that competition is of itself a good thing, that it invariably produces excellence, leads to a striving for perfection, invokes ambition even in the indolent, rewards the winners, spurs the losers on to greater things, represents virtue, embraces fairness, clean-cut camaraderie, with handshakes all round at the end, and all the other tosh I stopped believing when I gave up reading comics. The truth of the matter is that competition may indeed do all or some of those things, but it can also be dirty, underhand, demoralising for the loser, inhibiting of performance and, what is worse, thoroughly unfair.

I remember first seeing this sleazy side when, as an impressionable lad, I entered a pop group competition in the North-east. Having been told only where the theatre was and that Geordies were Scotsmen with their brains kicked in, we duly turned up for rehearsals and discovered that the result of the competition was a foregone conclusion. One outstanding group with a phenomenal lead guitarist was so impressive the rest of us just wanted to go home and forget the whole idea.

On the night, however, one of his nastier rivals tweaked the peg of the lead guitarist's top string as he went on stage, and he spent all his time playing a semitone lower than the rest or trying to retune his guitar. It sounded like Stravinsky on a bad day and his group came nowhere.

Unfortunately much of the Government's faith in competition is misplaced. Take the assumption that children will compete to produce better scores on national tests and that the standard of work will therefore improve. Some will indeed strive to outperform their fellows, but if the climate becomes too competitive people rapidly develop effective defences.

One possibility is simply to opt out, refuse to take part, in some cases under-perform. Another defence is to immunise oneself by detaching from reality. I remember a few years ago my own favourite football team, Sheffield Wednesday, was firmly anchored at the bottom of the Third Division. When they played against the next to bottom club an intrepid band of spectators at both ends, whose average IQ would have doubled had one placed a potted plant in their midst, kept up an incessant chant throughout the game of "we are the champions". Habitual winners thrive most on competition, losers have a different fate.

The reason why standards of achievement have improved in the GCSE is not because of competition, but rather because the nature of the examination changed. This allowed children to put greater effort into work that was, in general, more meaningful. Also there was due recognition of what had been achieved during the course, not just a single measurement of performance at the end. These factors outweighed the competitive instinct.

It is not only children who vary in their desire to outsmart the rest. Few teachers would kill for an incentive allowance. Well, I can think of one, but then he would kill for a bag of chips. One of the assumptions underlying merit payments is that people will strive to beat their colleagues in the rush for one. Yet collaboration is often much more important than competition among a school staff.

One of the aspects I find most worrying at the present time is competition between types of school. We now have three groups, in supposedly fair competition with each other — the maintained schools, the independents and the newly created semi-independent sector consisting of the city technology colleges and the grant maintained schools which have opted out of local authority control. Anyone who believes that this is a truly fair competition should think again.

Although I have never felt the need to send my own three children to independent schools as they have happily attended maintained schools, I have always held back from supporting those who would abolish all independent schools, though I have never understood how the poorest manage to extract cash from parents without actually using a sawn-off shotgun.

What dismays me, however, is first of all the claim that, because children in independent schools sometimes do better at exams than those in maintained schools, this is evidence of superior teaching. In fact it is often merely a reflection of smaller classes and the fact that independent schools deal mainly with some of the most socially privileged children, while maintained schools must teach everyone irrespective of wealth.

A further concern is the aggressive advertising pursued by some independent schools. The best seek good relationships with neighbouring maintained schools, but some attempt to do them down. The latest example even uses *not* having to teach the national curriculum as a selling point.

After stating that parents are flocking to independent schools in droves it goes on to say why: "The compulsory national curriculum, regular national testing, formal appraisal of teachers and greater parental control will benefit state education in time, but time, parents fear, is something that today's children do not have". In other words, come to us here where teachers are not buried by state bureaucracy.

Most worrying of all is the rigged competition between the semi independent sector and maintained schools. The millions of pounds of public money given to the city technology colleges is an utter disgrace. The Nottingham CTC alone received more money for buildings than all the schools in Leeds and Sheffield put together.

Equally bad is the amount of building money given to the grant maintained schools. I remember writing two years ago that these schools would be favoured, to encourage more to opt out, and that it would be like a race between two athletes, one in a Government-provided sports car, the other with his ankles tied to the starting gate. The average amount of building money given by the Government to maintained schools is £15,000 each. The average given to the 29 schools which have so far opted out is £226,000 each.

When these sums were announced the DES spokesman appeared to struggle for words to explain why the latter should receive *fifteen* times as much as the former. Perhaps I can help out with a few words that he dared not utter. Let's try bribery, chicanery, complete swizz, sharp practice, slippery, crooked, unworthy, insidious, infamous, shifty, unscrupulous, diabolical liberty, sick as a parrot and "We are the champions", for a start.

My next trick is impossible

In the early 1950s I was taken to witness what turned out to be, though we did not realise it at the time, the death throes of the Music Hall. I am glad my childhood was enhanced by the experience. Ever since seeing Stan Laurel and Oliver Hardy on their last tour of Britain I have realised that Music Hall never really died. Half the performers were taken on by television and the other half went into the House of Commons.

The classic combination of the famous comedy duo lives vividly in the memory. Both were inept in their different ways, the one greasy and obsequious, smiling effusively on the surface, but intemperate privately, the other terminally bewildered, looking likely to burst into tears at the next mishap. It was amazing that Kenneth Baker and Angela Rumpty Tumpty actually got the 1988 Education Act through Parliament.

One of the most impressive turns was somebody whose name I forget now, perhaps it was Marvo, for I think he may have done a bit of magic as well, perhaps it was Bob Dunn, who knows. Anyway Marvo, or whoever, had what was billed as a "talking dog" and was so clever, the audience was told, that he could actually do arithmetic on stage. Perhaps that rules out the Cabinet minister.

Marvo would proceed to ask his dog to do a sum, like ten take away two. The amazing talking Cabinet minister would then obediently bark eight times. This utterly astonished the audience, my youthful gullible self included, who were not aware that all Marvo did was tell the stupid mongrel when to stop barking via a secret signal. Nowadays the Prime Minister's Press secretary does that sort of thing.

Marvo's amazing talking dog seems to me to have been a real trend-setter so far as the national curriculum is concerned. I make it that he must have been performing at level 2 of maths attainment target 3 (compare two numbers to find the difference), and near enough at level 2 of English attainment target 1 (talk with the teacher, listen and answer questions).

I suppose today's demanding television audiences would expect him to cover all the topics in the proposed history syllabus as well, from Plato to

116

NATO, including "Japan and the Shogunate", whatever that is. I thought it must be an oriental rock group. Incidentally, if Marvo can get his dog as far as level 2 of the national curriculum, perhaps someone should sign him up as a licensed teacher — Marvo that is, not the dog, though if the teacher shortages get any worse the mongrel will no doubt be needed to teach 3C before too long.

What set me thinking about Marvo's amazing dog was not so much the national curriculum, but rather the emphasis there seems to be nowadays on "performance". There is something of Marvo's dog about the word that I never liked when it applied to teaching. It must be the uneasy feeling that a "performance" in teaching suggests being the agent of command rather than acting autonomously. The word also connotes what the *Oxford Dictionary* calls 'ridiculous or contemptible behaviour". It is all rather too empty-headed for something as thoughtful as skilled teaching.

At a time when public services like education and health care are dominated by the language and precepts of the accountant, however, terms like "performance indicator" take on special significance. Some of the more knuckle-headed accountants firmly believe that all human activity can be quantified in cash terms. A list of performance indicators can therefore be drawn up, it is argued, which shows how cost-effective each activity or institution is. For example, the teaching cost per pupil, the amount of money spent on books, the scores of children in tests can be computed and comparisons then made between different schools.

A doctor was telling me recently how much the medical profession resents performance indicators being applied to their own activities. If you were to take as an indicator of performance how many patients actually snuff it during treatment, this would be bad news for those working with the terminally ill but terrific news for those on the ingrowing toenail ward.

The same reservations apply to the use of performance indicators in education. It is another sad legacy from the Bun era that the DES still has an appetite to judge schools and teachers by performance indicators. Yet the crude use of test scores, the futility of comparing heating costs in two schools built a century apart, the utter folly of some indicators that have been proposed, like "crime rates in the area", should all, by now, have combined to see off the whole idea in its silliest form. It is analogous to judging the skill of ballet dancers by measuring their height.

Even worse is the proposal to reward heads by performance related pay. One indicator suggested was the truancy rate in the school: the more truants the less pay. This will be received ecstatically by the governors of Parkhurst,

Sing Sing, Devil's Island and the director of your local cemetery, most of whom have little trouble on the absentee front.

I suspect Bun is just too busy nowadays to reflect on the performance indicator farce. He seems to spend most of his time telling the press how extraordinarily correct the Prime Minister is in all her decisions, and occasionally hinting, if the tide is turning, that he has had a firm word with her, just to remind everybody what a macho guy he really is and what a fine Prime Minister he would make.

If John MacGregor ever does stop on the corridors of the Palace of Varieties to exchange pleasantries about performance indicators with Marvo's dog, perhaps he will utter the immortal words that said it all, "Here's another fine mess you've gotten me into Stanley".

And all because the DES loves...

There is a logical consequence of the market-mad philosophy which dominates education at present. It is that schools should advertise themselves. The marketeers who favour the educating-children-is-like-selling-cans- of-beans viewpoint argue that, if maintained schools are in competition with the independent sector, then they will have to use whatever means are available to peddle their wares.

When the first city technology college was established, Mr Bun, no slouch at advertising himself, in every sense of that phrase, was said to be delighted that the heads of the maintained schools in the area had had to spend more time and money publicising their own schools. I suspect they would have been happier spending it more directly on classroom needs, but this is regarded as a wimpishly uncommercial view.

So far as advertising is concerned, schools are getting themselves into a curious world with its own conventions, fashions and language. Will parents be told that their children will acquire a "ring of confidence", or that GCSE maths reaches the parts that other subjects cannot reach? There is not likely to be too much call for Drinka Pinta Milka Day since Miss Piggy ensured a few years ago that schools have no longer Gotta Lotta Bottle.

There was a campaign a few years ago to attract more recruits into the navy, based on the slogan, "It's a great life in the navy". Sailors were shown playing football, sunbathing on a tropical beach, anything other than killing people or spending six weeks at the bottom of the ocean in a submarine. Don't expect to see too many teachers marking books all evening, dealing with disruptive pupils or negotiating an overdraft in the DES's "It's a great life in the secondary school" film.

There might be some mileage in redesigning those car adverts that stress new technology: "The Education Act: designed by dummies, tested by robots", followed by the Plowden Report being hurled through a first-floor window. There will not be too many heads rushing to resurrect the "Wot-a-lot-I-got" slogan, however, though my old friends, the British Egg Information Service, might want to recycle the "Go to work on an egg-ocentric national curriculum" campaign.

I wonder whether there will be any place for what is usually called "knocking copy", with which advertisers seek to decry their Brand X competitors. I doubt if we shall see "Little Piddlington primary school gets a lot better type of pupil than some schools we could mention", or "Tests have shown that nine out of ten parents prefer Swinesville comprehensive", but some independent school advertising has sailed perilously close to that style in recent years.

There ought to be some possibilities in tobacco advertising, not too much of the gold or purple silk, of course, but I have always been convinced that the poor beggar in the cigar advert who endures every conceivable misfortune, before settling down to his six-pack, must be a teacher. No one else could be that unlucky.

The scene could start with the teacher missing out on an incentive allowance, then being asked to write a report on the national curriculum statutory order in maths, and finally being replaced by a licensed teacher because the governing body is eager to save money. Camera cuts to teacher sitting in empty staffroom smoking last cigar in six-pack to the accompaniment of Bach's *Air on the G string.*

Then there is that rich seam of aggressive macho ads showing heroic figures leaping across chasms, crossing flooded rivers to deliver the product.

Perhaps we shall see Mr Bun swinging along on a rope, closing down the Burnham Committee, rejecting the Higginson Report on A- levels, booting out the European Lingua programme, and finally planting a copy of the teachers' conditions of service contract on Miss Piggy's bedside table, to the slogan, "And all because the lady loves — Dismay".

On the other hand, this last macho-style ad may not be wholly convincing in the light of Edward Heath's recent comment that Mr Bun and Douglas Hurd are "scared stiff" of the Prime Minister. Perhaps, in real life, when Miss Piggy is giving a massive hand bagging to the Cabinet, Bun is either quivering under the table or hanging by his fingertips from the windowsill outside the room. I bet he doesn't drink Carling Black Label.

Spectre of debt is real hardship

The proposal to offer loans to students instead of grants has alarmed me ever since it was first discussed. I suspect I would never have had the privilege of four years at university if the consequence had been a huge debt at the end of it.

Let those who benefit from higher education pay the proper price, it is argued. Yet many graduates take modestly-paid jobs in public service, relatively few enjoying the vast yuppie richesse of which so much has been written.

If that is the case, supporters of loans argue, these should be top-up loans, not the full cost charge, and a repayment schedule should be devised which is related to earnings, so that impoverished graduates pay little until they are earning at a higher level.

But deferred payment assumes greater significance the longer the delay. It affects women in particular, when they wish to start their family, or puts the squeeze on men at the very time when their wives have stopped work and they have young children to support. This spectre of being impecunious at some future date can be felt as keenly as the reality of present financial hardship.

The puniest argument for me is that if students are really motivated they will take vacation jobs and "work their way through college" as happens in the United States. This may be possible for someone in the better-off South-east, but is not so feasible in the North, Scotland, Wales and Northern Ireland, where regular workers have enough problems finding decently-paid employment, let alone casual workers.

The real winners would be better-off parents. Many take out a bank loan or increase their mortgage to see their children through university. They almost certainly pay a higher commercial rate of interest than under a government-sponsored scheme.

The losers would be working-class children and the less well-off. The prospect of a significant debt stretching into an uncertain future for someone with no tradition of higher education in the family would put off all but the most unusually determined.

Supporters of loans argue that, since only a quarter of university students come from outside the two highest social classes, this small group can only increase. It has been a highly significant quarter and it would, I fear, go down to little or nothing.

A few years ago I took part in a BBC radio discussion on student loans. Every bank manager in the audience, contrary to the expectations of the BBC producer who had seated them on the "in favour" side of the audience, strongly opposed loans, each able to supply horror stories of earnest graduates on their books struggling to pay off loans.

I stand by a fair system of grants underwritten by taxpayers able to pay for and reap the benefits of producing a strong cohort of graduates from rich and poor families. It is, I fear, becoming an old-fashioned romantic stance.

Let's play spot the minister

In 1992 European frontiers, so far as the Economic Community is concerned, are to be thrown open. Stop the average Brit in the street and ask about 1992 and the answer you are most likely to get is that it is the date of the next Olympics.

Professions like engineering and medicine have given considerable thought to the open recognition of professional qualifications, which will be a requirement after 1992. In education there has scarcely been a whisper about teachers being able to teach anywhere in the Community.

There are going to be some real problems. In many European countries there is no proper teacher training system at all. In Greece, for example, the minister must not only recognise anyone with any modest academic award as a qualified teacher, but must also find him or her a job in a school. Now you know where Kenneth Baker got his licensed teacher scheme from.

The hope has been expressed by some people that in 1992 all our teacher shortage problems will be solved. The frontiers will open, it is said, and thousands of well qualified Germans, all speaking perfect English, will flood in to fill the maths and science vacancies. The not-so-well qualified are never mentioned, nor is the likelihood of movement in the other direction.

When British teachers look closely at the salaries and conditions in German schools a fair number of them will be tempted to move there to teach English, as some already do. Far from gaining teachers we might see a net loss, especially in the vital field of English and modern languages.

I have always said that I find students absolutely terrific nowadays. Many of them are the best of their generation. What higher education will be like in the 1990s, when vouchers and loans have turned it into a collection of Yuppiversities, is anybody's guess.

The various government plans and leaks are bad news for poorer and less privileged children. In future it is likely that students will be financed partly by bank loans. The prospect of finishing a course several thousand pounds in debt is not going to be attractive for the children from areas of high unemployment.

The only bright spot of the week was a sight which greeted me when Robert Jackson, junior minister responsible for higher education, visited my university to give a lecture. As ever students throughout the region decided to picket the event, and various mini-bus loads duly arrived.

Alas, once more the old saying that most students could not organise a knees-up in a brewery was perfectly fulfilled. One group arrived an hour too soon and wandered round the campus asking people if they had seen Robert Jackson anywhere, because no-one had told them the time and place of the lecture.

Another group spotted a police car outside the great hall and took up their position, complete with banner, to chant "Out, out, out," at the hundreds of people entering the building. If the latter looked completely mystified it was because they had only come to attend the British Legion's annual festival.

Biting the bullet takes the biscuit

So Saatchi and Saatchi is to mount a £2.2 million Government- sponsored advertising campaign to try to recruit more teachers. Since Angela Rumpty Tumpty has been going round saying there is no such thing as a teacher shortage, why is the Government spending this huge sum rectifying a problem which apparently does not exist?

Could this mean more money for non-existent problems? Perhaps there will be millions of pounds given to schools to buy books and equipment they already have, mend roofs that don't leak, paint walls that were only painted last week, and pay teachers even more money than the fortune they now earn.

I got wind of this new advertising development a few weeks ago. On returning from a visit to a school I found a note on my desk saying, 'A man from Saatchi and Saatchi phoned. He will ring back." He never did, but I fancy he must have wanted me to come up with a few snappy slogans, the odd alluring visual image, perhaps even star in the TV commercials as 'Deliriously happy of Exeter", the man who only finds true fulfilment when faced with 5d on a wet Friday afternoon.

Although advertisers themselves would make much more grandiose claims, the principal purpose of advertising is to deceive. There are certain exceptions, where the chief intention is to inform, but in the majority of cases the thrust of an advertising campaign is to persuade people that one's product is better than that of the competitors, even if it is not. Television commercials do not usually begin, " Remember our competitors' products are not only better than our own, but also more fairly priced". If they did we should immediately be suspicious that there was a catch, and some clever strategy was about to be deployed.

One of the main aims of the campaign, according to the Department of Education and Science, is to counter the negative image of teachers and teaching frequently portrayed in newspapers. This could be an especially difficult assignment, given the consistently critical line adopted by some of the press.

It is not uncommon for journalists to find favourable stories spiked, especially of teaching in comprehensive schools, simply because the newspaper concerned is unwilling to publish. As often as not, therefore, the journalist will not even bother to write anything favourable in the first place. There is such a history of negative images that even a prolonged and sophisticated campaign may achieve little.

There are many styles in advertising, and it will be interesting to see which one Saatchi and Saatchi adopts. One favoured device is that of "knocking copy", where you find your biggest rivals and put the boot into them, the "not like some cars we could mention" or "Brand X" approach.

Given that many graduates are being attracted into the City nowadays, this might be difficult. The opening words could be: "If you think that going off in your Porsche to an expensive hotel in the South of France is more fun than loading up the boot of your Hillman Imp with 150 books to mark over the weekend, you couldn't be more wrong." I can't see it myself.

One of the most seductive approaches, which pushes right against the very edge of the code of advertising standards, highlights the popularity which will accrue from owning the product, the purchaser being shown surrounded by a crowd of admirers, usually of the opposite sex. The scene here would show a teacher lolling casually on the edge of a bar with some matinee idol calling to his mates, "Hey, fellers, come over here, this lady's a *teacher*". Over would rush a squad of handsome men to admire her flat brogues and ask her how she managed to meet all the attainment targets of the national curriculum. I can't see that one either. If they did all rush across it would probably be to play hell with her for not being able to afford her round on the princely salary she's being paid.

Another possibility is to dream up an appealing slogan that will enter the public consciousness, alongside "You'll smell a little lovelier each day" and "Everyone's a fruit and nut case", both of which come to think of it, might be used as they stand. The British Airways line "We'll take good care of you" might have a hollow ring to it in the present climate, but then I never believed the original either.

Since some local authorities are also running their own campaigns, it might be necessary to devise a few locally flavoured slogans. Fry and Laurie could do their double act, where one is the ultra-clever marker of children's work and the other ticks all the wrong boxes, to the catch phrase. "You get a better Tester teaching in Leicester". More realistic would be "Just shake 'n' vac", given that, with not enough money for cleaners, some teachers may be sweeping up their own classrooms.

Perhaps the most fruitful approach would be to model the whole campaign on banking adverts. The style here is to suggest that you, the customer, are really super-shrewd, and that the dark suited bank officials are gullible dupes. The typical setting shows a professional couple or a spotty youth, depending on the target of the ads, interviewing a bank manager or two and demanding a special set of facilities which they eventually get. The end of the scene portrays a triumphant customer and a rattled-looking banker pretending he has been taken to the cleaner's. In reality there is nothing special about the account facilities on offer, and in certain cases the truth is that the same or a better deal could be obtained elsewhere.

Perhaps the dialogue in the teacher recruitment version could go like this, as urbane DES official chats to callow would-be teacher in some plush office setting:

"So you want a job with long hours?"
And plenty of unpaid overtime."
(Raises eyebrows) "And unpaid overtime?"
That's right. Oh, and I'd like to be slagged off regularly by
politicians and newspapers."
"Hm, regular slagging as well." (Makes notes)
"Yes, that's double 'l' in 'Wally', by the way. And while you're on
with it I want to spend most of my time filling in forms and scoring
tests rather than teaching."
*(Gulps)"Scoring tests, I see. (Looking bashful). Would you like a
biscuit?"*
So it's a deal then?"
"No, that's your first month's salary."

Real men don't need Baker's PR

A bizarre story appeared in the press a couple of weekends ago. Three Cabinet ministers, David Waddington, Kenneth Clarke and Secretary of State for Education John MacGregor, were each going to be given their own senior public relations consultant to help improve their image.

Read on, I thought to myself, gripped by that uneasy feeling one has when the chip pan is about to catch fire. The individual consultant, to be called "special communications adviser," would, it transpired, work intensively with the Minister concerned to help improve his and his department's image.

Never mind the chip pan, by now the smell was distinctly fishy so I read further. Before long all was revealed: "The idea to give the ministers such advisers arose from a dinner hosted six weeks ago by the Tory Party chairman, Kenneth Baker, and attended by five senior advertising and public relations figures". "Enough said, squire.

Can you imagine the effect on poor old John MacGregor? I wonder how he found out, assuming he was actually told. Perhaps the phone rang, and a voice said, "Hello John, it's Kenneth Baker here. Look, I've decided to help you improve your image so that you can be as popular with teachers as I was". To do that to a man who, in a previous post, was presumably rung up and told, "And the name of your new junior minister is — Edwina Currie", was all too unfair, more than any one man should be asked to bear, a confirmation of life's many cruelties.

As a message that must have chilled him to the marrow, it probably ranks with such historical pronouncements as, "Hello, Mrs Caesar. Brutus and I just thought we'd pop round with a few friends for a chat with your Julius" or perhaps, "Dad, it's Vlad the Impaler. Something about you being behind with the rent", or even, "Do you think those Indians are waving at us, General Custer?"

There were signs of retreat on the plan this week, so perhaps Mac has been spared the knife. But why change the poor beggar's image at all? All right, so he may sometimes look a bit like that disposable bit actor on *Star Trek,* whose resigned expression early in the programme tells you that he realises

128

his sole function in the episode is to be beamed down on to the planet Zarg and turned into a heap of white granules by the Klingons. And yes, he may sometimes bore viewers by saying, "If I may finish, Mr Dimbleby, there are just seven more points I'd like to make".

But at least he seems intelligent, thoughtful and willing to listen to professional opinion and take sensible action when the need arises, despite having been marooned waist deep in fertiliser by his predecessor. So why change a nice man into a Flash Harry, when there are enough spivs around in politics and too few real people? If I were John MacGregor, I would tell any new image-maker unambiguously and in the most precise anatomical detail, exactly where to stick his Brylcreem.

Ever since the Manpower Services Commission became involved in education I have enjoyed many a titter at the notions they sometimes brought with them in their baggage. The best has been very welcome and refreshing, the worst seriously out of place, slightly missing the right tone, a bit like a butcher wandering into a vegetarian restaurant and asking if anyone would like a juicy steak.

Now renamed the Training Agency and equipped with a new logo, showing what looks like a man with half his body trapped in a door, giving rise to new possibilities for the phrase "this will cost you an arm and a leg," their latest missive has just landed on my desk.

It is from an outfit known as the National Training Task Force which is running some National Training Awards Scheme for 1990. The letter is headed "An invitation to beat your competitors" and it invites me to win a "coveted" (by whom is not revealed) Training Award. It goes on, "And if you decide not to enter, some of your competitors probably will". Gosh, that will strike terror into the heart of the British education system.

The letter is signed by one Brian Wolfson who is chairman of Wembley Stadium. Now anyone who runs Wembley is all right by me, as some of the greatest moments in my life have been spent watching, albeit on television, football and other sports at that marvellous stadium. The chance to combine teacher training and football is just too good to miss Brian.

There are some problems, however. You see, teacher training has been a game of two halves, Brian. Up to about the mid 1970s the lads done great. We was over the moon Brian, plenty of keen recruits, loads of freedom to experiment with new formations. But in the last few years there's been not enough youngsters coming through. Now we've just been told we've got to fill in an *18 page* form in future for every single new course.

We can't play them off the park any longer Brian, because, like schools we're strangled by bureaucracy. So we take each game as it comes, play the full 90 minutes, give 200 per cent, deny them space, don't give the ball away, just keep it simple, play it to feet, compete for every ball, get stuck in, move forward in numbers, track back, find space, mark tight. Sorry not to enter your comp, but we're just gutted Brian, sick as a parrot.

Another strange story in the press recently was about the death of the Yuppie. Apparently advertisers have now lost interest in Yuppies and have instead turned their attention to "Yappies", which stands for Young Affluent Parents.

I feel we need this sort of easy memorable shorthand stereotyping for teachers nowadays, so I have been racking my brain to think of a few examples. There are those teachers who ingratiate themselves with senior management in a tireless quest for promotion, known as "Creepies" (Crawls Regularly and Exploits Every Possibility). Other groups worthy of media recognition include the people who can never say no to any request and have therefore earned the tag "Wallies" (Will always be Lumbered), and young teachers with families to support known as "Flossies" (Forget Leisure, Often Severely Skint).

Most deserving of all, however, is that squad of senior people, worn out by the heavy workload they carry. They have borne the brunt of all the ceaseless changes of the last few years and are due a well-earned rest. They will henceforth be known as "Sleepies" (Shattered, Listless, Exhausted and Extremely Pissed-off).

Join the Right and ring the changes

Have you ever fancied having your own Education Act? I mean your very own personalised designer Education Act, the 1992 Agnes Scattergood or the 1994 Alf Ramsbottom Education Act? I have been close a couple of times. Three years ago I was invited to Athens by the Greek Minister of Education. We spent a couple of days getting excited about the whole of Greek education, generating bright new ideas from nursery up to further and higher education. A fortnight later I heard that he had resigned.

The following year I was invited to Madrid by the Spanish Minister of Education to advise him about secondary schooling. A few months later I learned that he too had resigned. With such an impressive record as the architect of the Not the 1987 Greek Education Act and the Not the 1988 Spanish Education Act, plus a hundred per cent success at administering the kiss of death to any Minister who sought my advice, I sat patiently by the phone hoping fervently that Kenneth Baker would ring up for the odd tip. Unfortunately, Old Smarmy Boots, who was in any case as receptive to advice as the average jam jar, never called.

I now realise that if you want your own Education Act you must study carefully the tactics of those people who have provided the thinking, if that is not too ambitious a word, for recent legislation. There is a set of right-wing pressure groups that has got it off to a very fine art. Much of the content of recent legislation derives from the pamphlets of the Centre for Policy Studies, the Adam Smith Institute and similar groups.

Perhaps the origins of some of this lie with Ken Dodd and the Diddymen who are supposed to work down a jam butty mine in Knotty Ash. It may be that, deep underground, these groups assiduously dig for pamphlets in some seam rich with booklets lambasting maintained schools, or advocating the abolition of local authorities, Her Majesty's Inspectorate, and teacher training.

I have no doubt that their motives are sincere and that they genuinely seek to improve education. It is their strategies that are fascinating. For example, there are *several groups,* but the membership is similar. Centre for Policy

Studies papers often bear the same names as papers from the National Council for Educational Standards. When a New outfit calling itself the Hillgate Group appeared, there they were again in the pamphlets.

Once you have created several groups the next step is to *keep quoting one another.* Most of these pamphlets cite each other as authoritative sources, creating the impression that the whole world is of one mind. This is then allied to the big assertion. Rather than mess around with piddling claims, *go for the big one.*

Thus the Hillgate Group claim that people who work in teacher training seek to "subvert the entire traditional curriculum" and that this is "too well known to bear lengthy comment". This message is then picked up by the Centre for Policy Studies which claims that teacher-training courses only cover such matters as special educational needs, equal opportunities and multicultural education, what are called a random set of topics, because they fascinate educationists. In practice each of these is actually required by the Government and is spelled out in the relevant Department of Education and Science circulars governing the content of teacher-training courses.

Even some of the intellectually able right-wingers are not immune from the big assertion. Both Professor Anthony Flew and Professor Anthony O'Hear have made claims based on the same false argument. Anthony Flew believes that, because independent schools in general do better in public exams than maintained schools, all schools should be independent. Anthony O'Hear asserts that because many independent schools have untrained teachers, all teachers should be untrained.

Unfortunately the Two Tones are both wrong if they believe that "independentness" or "untrainedness" cause exam success. They seem not to have spotted that the seven per cent of pupils who attend the independent sector are from much more privileged backgrounds than the 90-plus per cent who go to maintained schools; that the money per pupil is often twice as high or more in the independent sector, leading to smaller classes and other benefits; or that most independent schools do hire trained teachers.

Another tactic is to *reach the big conclusion.* Thus the Hillgate Group concludes that the answer to all our problems is to have lots of untrained licensed teachers who, they claim, "will show up the inadequacies of many existing teachers and practices". All one then needs is *a come-on to the press,* like the Adam Smith Institute accusing primary schools of teaching a "Blue Peter curriculum."

Flooding schools with untrained licensed teachers certainly would show existing teachers, a thing or two, like how to teach with three children sitting on your chest. Anyway, I dread to think what a really right-wing curriculum would look like: period 1, spelling; period 2, spelling; period 3, even more spelling; period 4, spelling test; period 5, that's enough spelling, let's do punctuation instead; period 6, the history and evolution of the semicolon; periods 7 and 8, yes, it's spelling time again children.

So if you've got the hang of it, you and I can now sit down and plan our very own DIY Education Act. First let's set up one or two groups we can belong to, preferably with neutral sounding titles. You have to watch the acronyms, which rules out the Centre for Really Advanced Policies, but let's settle for the Institute of Jolly Sensible Ideas and the British Association of Awfully Nice People.

Next we need a cause, so how about the teaching of the Tango, which as we all know has been greatly neglected in our schools. I myself, writing under the name Ding, in my IJSI pamphlet "The Great Non-Tango Scandal", will assert that teachers have deliberately omitted the Tango from the school curriculum. You under the name Dong in your BAANP pamphlet, "It takes Two to Tango", will echo this with, "As Ding and others have shown beyond any reasonable doubt..." going on to demand immediate action.

We then line up a couple of our mates, Bing and Bong, to confirm that the teaching profession, as Ding and Dong have demonstrated conclusively, is full of subversives who systematically undermine decent Tango teaching in this country, putting us at the bottom of the international Tango league. Ding, Dong, Bing and Bong have now proved beyond a shadow of a doubt that only an Education Act can save us. Fun this, isn't it? Ding Dong Bell.

Also from Trentham Books

THE WRAGGED EDGE: EDUCATION IN THATCHER'S BRITAIN

SWINESHEAD REVISITED

PEARLS FROM SWINESHIRE

These three volumes contain selections of Ted Wragg's most seminal articles on the state of education in modern Britain. All are written with his characteristic wit and style and have enjoyed widespread acclaim. Now gathered together, selected and edited by the author, they form a remarkably trenchant and coherent analysis of contemporary educational issues. Like all Ted Wragg's work the books appeal to readers who seek entertainment as well as those committed to serious study.

■ "Wragg's style is a constant delight. Education should be grateful to have him around". — *Education Today.*

■ "His essays are above all a good read, and perhaps a morale booster for those who feel they may be running out of energy to keep on fighting". — *Education Guardian.*

Swineshead Revisited
ISBN: 9507735 2 2
Price £3.95. 122 pages, A5

Pearls from Swineshire
ISBN: 0 948080 05 1
Price £3.95. 122 pages, A5

The Wragged Edge
ISBN: 0 948080 21 3
Price £6.95, 128 pages, A5

Trentham Books Limited
13/14 Trent Trading Park
Botteslow Street
Stoke-on-Trent
England ST1 3LY

tb